THERE'S ONE BORN EVERY MINUTE

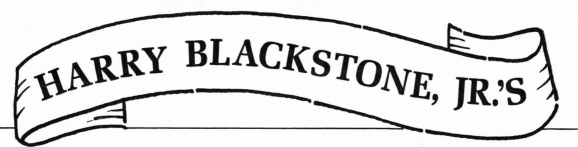

HARRY BLACKSTONE, JR.'S

THERE'S ONE BORN EVERY MINUTE

Edited by Leo Behnke

JEREMY P. TARCHER, INC.
Los Angeles
Distributed by Houghton Mifflin Company
Boston

Library of Congress Cataloging in Publication Data

Blackstone, Harry.
    There's one born every minute.

    Summary: A magician shares his collection of "betchas,"
or tricks that another person would be willing to bet
you could not do, along with techniques for setting up
these unlosable bets.
    1. Tricks. [1. Tricks. 2. Magic tricks. 3. Card
tricks] I. Behnke, Leo. II. Title.
GV1547.B625 1984   793.8   84-8477
ISBN 0-87477-329-6

Jeremy P. Tarcher, Inc.
9110 Sunset Blvd.
Los Angeles, CA 90069

Designed and illustrated by The Committee

Manufactured in the United States of America
D 10 9 8 7 6 5 4 3

Table of Contents

3. Scientific Principles 55

Introduction

Socrates (who never expected to be quoted in a book like this) and all the major philosophers from ancient times to the present have said that the greatest wisdom a man could have was to "know himself." P.T. Barnum (who might have sued if we had not brought up his name) felt that the greatest wisdom a man could have was the recognition that "there's a sucker born every minute." They may well have been talking about the very same thing, for a sucker is somebody who doesn't know himself. He is unaware of his own ignorance, and indeed often mistakes his ignorance for knowledge. It is just that mistake that makes him a sucker, for he is ready to bet against a smarter—if not a better—man, even when it should be apparent to him that the other guy knows something he doesn't.

It is on this universal and unchanging fact that this book is based. As a magician, and the son of a magician, I've seen people fooled by magic tricks for years and years. But magic, although it fools an audience, doesn't *make* fools of the audience because everyone knows in advance that he is about to be tricked, and only a very few believe that they know how the trick was done and could do it themselves. That is exactly the opposite of the approach to the tricks—which we call *betchas*—that you'll find in this book. The audience (usually only one

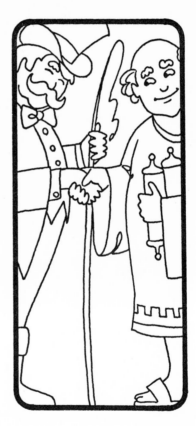

person) becomes a participant in a trick which he is convinced is not a trick, just a terrible misstatement or a vain boast that you have made and that he is now going to make you wish you hadn't. I guarantee that's the way it works . . . almost every time!

I must tell you that you are getting these betchas cheap. Oh, I know you paid for this book (at least, I hope you did!), but what I put into this collection cost me years of study, patience, self-denial, extraordinary humiliation, and more dollars than I care to think about. And you're getting the benefit of this all at once. Some people have all the luck.

I'm not only giving you the betchas but, equally important, I'll suggest how to word many of them so that the other person will bite at the line you are dangling so temptingly in front of him. And, in addition to these almost unlosable bets, I've put in a chapter on figuring the odds which, even if it doesn't change your luck, will show you exactly why you're losing and that it has nothing to do with the fact that you forgot to wear your lucky yellow socks.

Now, although among people who delight in issuing these little challenges the challenged person is known variously as the victim, sucker, dupe, or mark, we hesitate to use the same blatant terminology. Henceforth, this book will designate the challenged person as the *student*. After all, aren't you, the teacher, about to let this person pay for the privilege of gaining higher beneficial knowledge? And many are the times I've seen a student who has just been educated go out and within five minutes get his buck back from someone else.

But the main thing is that betchas are a lot of fun. No one minds losing a dollar or a few coins if they are entertained at the same time. I admit that when you show or give the answer to some of these you'll hear a few groans, and might even get a fishy stare from the assembled multitude, but a little bit of that kind of treatment has always been the fate of genius. So, go out and regardless of whether you issue these challenges for bucks, wooden nickels, or just to exhibit what a truly knowledgeable person you are, I betcha have lots of fun. . .

Harry Blackstone, Jr.

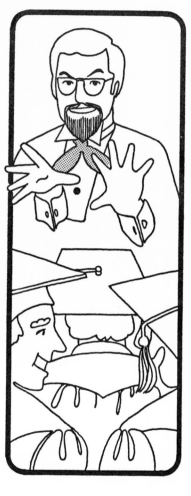

Setting It Up
Steering the Conversation

The first thing to know about betchas is that they have to be set up with care. Oh, occasionally you'll get the opportunity to drop one of your challenges or untoppable bets into the normal flow of the conversation, but for the most part you'll have to steer it just a bit in the direction you want it to take. Along with the techniques for getting your student's attention so he becomes interested in your proposition, you have to learn how to phrase it and, if it requires a demonstration, you must be able to perform it. None of these is really difficult, so let's deal with first things first.

Getting Your Student's Attention

One of the very important members of a confidence-game gang is the fellow called a "steerer." He's the one who guides the victim to the action and sets him in the proper mood. Since you don't have anyone working with you, it's up to you to handle this yourself. To do this you use certain conversational devices as openers:

"That's nothing, I used to have an uncle who . . ."
"Kids are a lot smarter these days . . ."
"Boy, this modern world is fantastic . . ."
"Have you noticed that they're making . . ."
"I don't care, that's a lot of hooey!"

"I saw one once that was the (biggest, smallest, fastest, etc) . . . "

"Skill has nothing to do with it, I'm the luckiest . . . "

"Luck has nothing to do with it, I'm the best . . . "

Each of these sentences, like dozens of others you can devise, starts you off on what appears to be an exaggerated claim of some kind. As any teacher will tell you, the more outrageous your claim, the more likely you are to get your student's attention, and the more likely he is to doubt anything you say after it. What you want to do is put him in a mood of disbelief, and exaggeration—if you don't have to live up to it—will do just that.

For instance, imagine someone coming up to you and saying, "I just got back from a wonderful trip to Venus." You'd certainly listen to the next sentence out of his mouth, but I doubt that you'd believe it. If he later tells you some fact about Venus that seems totally improbable, you might well challenge it, even though he got the fact from an encyclopedia. The point is, his initial comment set you up to doubt anything else he said.

With a little practice and some attention to the individual's own expertise, you'll find that getting the other guy to listen to your proposition is a snap. Here (and throughout the book) I'll give you some examples of the way I do it. Make up your own; it's half the fun of betchas.

Another way to lead your student into your classroom is by tickling his curiosity, by nudging his pride, or by kicking his ego—where everyone is sensitive. Challenge a man particularly in an area where he thinks of himself as being expert and one where he knows you aren't, and chances are he'll take up a challenge that he wouldn't take under almost any other circumstances. Start a sentence with, "I never met an athlete who was as well co-ordinated as . . ." or "Accountants may know about profit and loss, but without their calculators they're a bunch of . . . " or "What's the matter with you? My five-year-old kid can . . . " and you are well on your way to getting your student to put up his home to show just how wrong you are.

For example, bet an English teacher that you can reel off a thousand words without once using the letter "a" and you've almost certainly got someone who will take you up on the boast, since he knows that "a" is the third most frequently used letter in the alphabet, and reeling off a hundred words without using an "a" is quite an accomplishment. What your English teacher friend (student) doesn't know is that you are about to count from 1 to 999, and there are no "a's" in the number system until you get to 1000. I guarantee you'll never get there. Long before you hit 100 your now wiser friend will have taken out his wallet and gladly paid you to stop counting. Don't worry, he'll pick up the money from his class the next time it meets.

If you know someone who thinks he knows his math, bet him about odds; bet an athletic friend to accomplish something physical; bet your best friends

who know you don't know anything about almost any subject, and almost without fail they will take you up on your challenge.

After a bit of practice, you'll find that you can take whatever subject you are talking about and, with a few verbal twists and turns, steer the conversation right to the point where your student will say, "I'll bet you're wrong." And then, my friend, you got 'im.

Stating Your Proposition

Up to now we've just been preparing the student mentally. Now we are, in reality, opening the door of the trap. This is the crucial moment. If your approach is too formal and awkward or your student hears the wrong words, he'll know you're laying a trap for him. Naturalness and casualness are essential. Be patient. The more you are able to choose the right moment instead of forcing the situation, the less likely you are to raise suspicion.

Using the right words to present the proposition is of the utmost importance. If you don't phrase it correctly the student will either figure it out for himself or will be able to catch you in your own trap. You need to get all the necessary conditions into the statement, tell the truth, and yet phrase it so your student is concentrating on one part of the proposition while it's actually some other part that has the important information.

For example, take the following fact. If you accordion-pleat a dollar bill into three vertical sections and fasten it with two paper clips, like the illustrations A and B, when you pull the two top corners of the bill the paper clips will not only fly off the bill but will become linked in the process! Now, how can you make this unlikely fact into a money-making proposition?

Since the linking of the paper clips is the most startling part, you should completely ignore any words that give that connotation when you give the challenge. Let's say the subject of skill or coordination or probability, or anything else remotely touching on the objects involved, comes up in conversation. You can, using the basic exaggeration technique, put it like this: "I saw a demonstration on TV of some guys shooting arrows. They were pretty good, but I remember when I was a kid we used to make catapults out of paper and paper clips, and just with that we could have outshot those champs."

At this point you remove a bill from your pocket, fold it in half, slip a paper clip (which you just happened to have in your change pocket) over the center of the fold as in C, and then jerk the ends of the bill open. The clip flies along the bar (or table, if you're with your relatives) just like an arrow from a bow. Repeat this move as you make the following statement: "But I was the best! They should have my name in the *Guinness Book of World Records*. I bet I can still do the Robin Hood thing . . . you remember, where he could split one arrow with a second one? Well, I bet I can still shoot two paper clips off this bill and wind up with them touching each other."

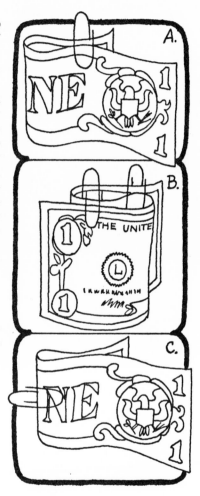

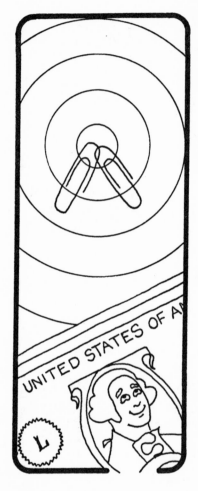

Notice how you have said nothing untruthful (except possibly about what you used to do as a kid) in the proposition—just that you'd shoot two paper clips off the bill and that they would be touching each other when you finished. You have to understand the phrasing completely in your mind because sometimes someone will repeat the bet back to you, or will have you phrase it another way. You must be able to say the same thing two or three different ways without leaving anything out or making a misstatement. Also, most important, notice that the statement doesn't say a word about shooting the two clips separately. You shot the original paper clip by itself and then immediately began to talk about shooting two paper clips. This is the crux of the whole proposition. If you mention *anything* to give the idea that two clips are to be shot at the same time you will create suspicion and you won't get a bet. Even when you put the two clips on the bill there isn't a thing to give them a clue about what's going to happen; just make sure you don't say a word about it ahead of time.

"Okay you guys, here goes, I'll double up the bill . . . put on a paper clip . . . fold it again and put on the second clip . . . and POW! You see, two paper clips touching each other even though they flew two feet through the air. Sure, I know they're linked—I just did that to show you not to fool around with Old Eagle-Eye."

Sometimes you can do the set-up with just words. Masking is another contrivance that often works wonders. What you do is set up a verbal smoke-screen, such a circuitous proposition that by the time you get to the end your listener has forgotten an essential fact you told him at the beginning. Take the following proposition for example.

An expert skier dreamed he was on a perfect vacation with his mother and his new bride. They were in the Swiss Alps with beautiful weather, perfect hiking conditions, and were having a wonderful time. Suddenly, a storm came up and stranded them on a small ledge high above the valley. Bit by bit, the stormy winds cut into the ledge, not only making the hikers miserable, but at the same time chipping away parts of the rock. As they watched, clutching each other for warmth and encouragement, bits and pieces of the shelf came loose and fell hundreds of feet into the rocky valley. Finally, the skier saw a way out. Just under one end of their narrow haven was a diagonal slope of snow, angling down the face of the mountain. The only problem was that it was a 10- or 12-foot drop down to the slope and, since he was the only one who had skis, it was a way out for only one or two people. Once he dropped down onto the slope he would be forced to glide down the side of the mountain, and there was no hope for the third person stranded on the ledge. His predicament—since he was the expert skier, had the only skis, and was the only one able to navigate that slope in that storm—was: who should he save, his wife or his mother? "Now," you say, "I've studied this problem ever since I first

heard it proposed and I think I have finally worked out the only true solution. A solution that will solve his predicament immediately, and I can give it in two words."

This long-winded story will immediately begin an equally long-winded and spirited debate among your audience. But when all the smoke has cleared and the clever ones turn to you in desperation for your answer, just tell them that you would tell the dreamer to *"Wake up!"*

You will see as you read this book that there are many different types of word traps in the Land of Betchas. Some of them depend on dual meanings, some on puns, others on the judicious use of synonyms or homonyms. Almost all utilize irrelevancy: emphasizing nonessential information, or hinting at a certain something that turns out to be a nothing. Whatever the form of your verbal deceit, you have to be able to follow up on your opening even if it's only a crack.

Use Your Head...and His

Using a little psychology here and there, you can easily strengthen your position. For example, suppose you have made an outrageous statement and received a halfhearted challenge—not quite a bet, but something close enough so that you know that with a little more prodding your student will take the bait. If you prod too hard, however, he may get suspicious. What do you do? You start to withdraw or modify the statement you made, appearing to back away from your prior commitment. For example, earlier you bet that the two paper clips would wind up touching each other. Your sucker almost bit, but he seems wary, so you say, "Well, I haven't practiced this in awhile and touching may be a little difficult for me. I'll bet that I can get them within a half inch of each other." Chances are he'll reply, "Oh, no, you said touching, and touching it's gotta be. Now let me see you do it." Of course, you're ready for him and once again, trickery, deceit, and dissembling lead to triumph! Or, in the proposition where you promised a thousand words without an "a," you might wish to cut that back to a hundred if the thousand seems to have been too many for your student to swallow all at once.

If the proposition requires the student to do something and he's doubtful of his ability to do it, be a sport. In the betchas in this book you'll learn the little secret that makes these challenges work and you can safely offer to do most of the tricks after he's failed.

Once he bites on the proposition, don't let him off the hook. Put some added pressure on him, especially if he is to perform some physical feat. Call some spectators over for the sport. Having a crowd will not make his work any easier, and that's the whole idea. Not only will an audience make him a little nervous, but you can use it to your advantage in other ways. For example, as soon as someone comes within range, repeat the bet and its conditions, and then turn to your student for verification. This

means you'll have reputable witnesses for the blow-off. Also, their heckling will tend to hurry and unnerve him, and surely that's not all bad.

The Payoff

One thing is certain—once in a while you will lose a bet, whether through carelessness or the fact that even when the odds are heavily in your favor it still doesn't mean you'll win 100 percent of the time. And sometimes your apparent student may turn out to be a lot more clever than you thought. Don't worry. The first thing you do in this appalling circumstance is not pay off. Always, but always, offer another proposition. It can be the same one if the odds warrant a repeat, or a different one that sounds like you're giving him an even better deal than you did the first time.

Since betchas are all in fun, it really doesn't matter whether he's won or lost. Your student will probably be ready for another challenge anyway. If he's lost, he'll welcome the opportunity to get even, and if he's won, he'll think he has your number. Well, maybe he had it once, but with this book to back you up the chances are he won't have it again.

One last word, this one about preparation. Many betchas that seem to be impromptu or done on the spur of the moment actually need a certain amount of preparation. Quite often the preparation is very simple and can be done long before you actually perform the bet, such as learning a knack or skill.

Others require a little devoted practice. The amount of time and effort devoted to perfecting a certain move is well worth the stunning effect it will have on your audience.

2. The Classics
Schoolboy and Bar Bets

We'll start off with some easy ones. The first dozen or so are the oldest and most common betchas I know and have probably been around since the snake bet Eve that she couldn't take just one bite. Still, many of them are just as good as the day they were first used, and as the title of this book says, "There's one born every minute."

As you read them notice the way the wording gives all the necessary information but at the same time tends to head the listener in the wrong direction.

The last group is also made up of very old catches, but they're not quite as common. Even in this day of instant communication and travel you'll find plenty of takers. But, then, that's good for you. It gives you a chance to go out and educate your fellow man!

Through the Hole

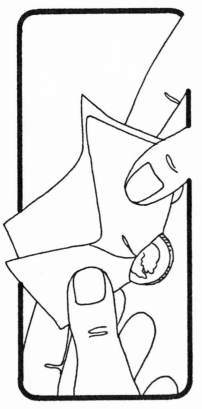

"Did you know that the biggest problem with sandwich-alloy coins is shrinkage? What do you mean, what do I mean? Do you have a quarter in your pocket? I'll cut a hole in this piece of paper the same size as a dime and push a quarter through that hole without tearing the paper. How much? For the quarter, of course."

If the student informs you that he already knows how to do this, ask him to demonstrate. He will do one of two actions, and you promptly tell him that his method is the way the kids do it in school and you have an entirely different technique. You now show him the alternate method, but get the money up front . . .

1. Put the quarter on the table, stick a pencil through the hole in the paper, and push the quarter with the pencil.

2. Fold the paper in half through the center of the hole and drop the quarter inside. Now hold each end of the crease and lever upward, using the hole as the center of the bend. The hole will stretch open and the quarter will drop through. Pick it up and drop it in your pocket.

Pushing Myself

A perfect follow-up to that last bet is this come-on.

"You think that was something? Listen, I can cut a hole in a business card and push my head through it without tearing the card."

When it comes time to accomplish the incredible, borrow a business card and a pair of scissors. Fold the card in half across its width. Make a cut down the center of the card from the folded edge to about 1/8 inch from the ends. Open the card and refold it, this time along the cut. Now from that cut edge make cuts toward the outside edges, placing them a little more than 1/4 inch apart, starting and finishing right at the ends of your long cut. Each cut stops about 1/8 inch from the outside edges. You should get about ten cuts. Turn the card around and now make cuts from the outside edges toward the center. Each cut is in between your first cuts, and each one stops 1/8 inch from the long cut running down the center of the card.

When you've finished, carefully open out the card, creasing each of the joints flat, and you'll have a lacy paper ring about 24 inches in circumference. If you can't get that over your head then your ego has been winning too many bets lately!

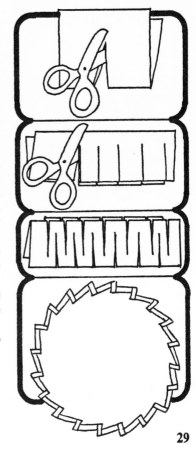

It's a Date

Any time a friend has a quarter you can get it for yourself by using the following ludicrous bet.

Take the quarter in your hand and, without looking at it, start rubbing it between your fingers. Finally, nod your head in satisfaction and give him back the quarter. "I'll bet you," you say, "that if you put a quarter face down in the palm of my hand, that just by looking at the tails side I can tell you the date."

The student obediently puts the quarter in your hand. You gaze intently at the coin, and then loudly call out the date of the day you are perpetrating this fraud. Don't forget to close your fist around the quarter that now belongs to you!

The Prisoner

You're sitting in a restaurant with a friend. Because you are such an elegant person, I know it will be a restaurant with tablecloths. The meal's over and you're about to leave the tip. As he takes the coins out of his pocket and puts them on the table you laugh.

"What's funny?" your friend says.

"Well, I was just remembering my Uncle Max who had this incredible ability to move objects without touching them. Even I can do it sometimes."

"That's ridiculous. I've known you for years and I've never seen you do anything like that."

"Okay, here's a dime on the tablecloth with a nickel on each side of it. I'm putting this glass upside down so its edge rests on the two nickels. Now, I'll bet you that dime that I can remove it from under that glass without touching the nickels or the glass."

Unless the student has a long memory he will probably bet you. At that point start scratching the tablecloth just outside the glass and the dime will walk right out to your waiting fingers.

Don't forget to leave another tip.

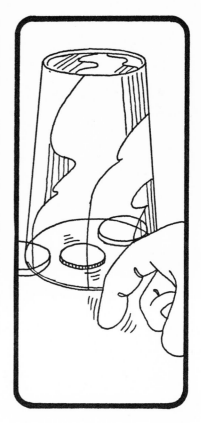

Moving Day

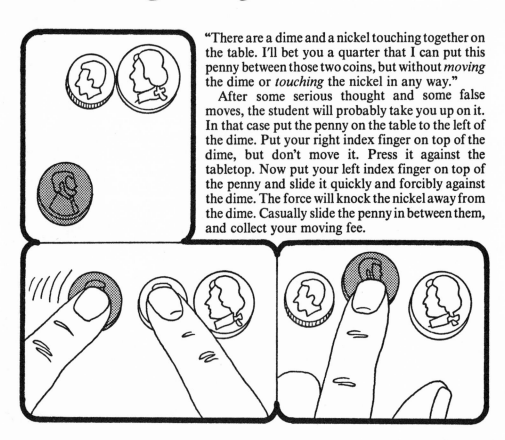

"There are a dime and a nickel touching together on the table. I'll bet you a quarter that I can put this penny between those two coins, but without *moving* the dime or *touching* the nickel in any way."

After some serious thought and some false moves, the student will probably take you up on it. In that case put the penny on the table to the left of the dime. Put your right index finger on top of the dime, but don't move it. Press it against the tabletop. Now put your left index finger on top of the penny and slide it quickly and forcibly against the dime. The force will knock the nickel away from the dime. Casually slide the penny in between them, and collect your moving fee.

Four from Eight

Here's a good example of the principle of irrelevancy. In other words, you introduce something that has nothing to do with the answer, but the student doesn't know that!

"Here's a pencil and a piece of paper. I bet I can take four away from four and leave eight. If you don't think so, just let me know for how much."

Once again you want to lean on the student a little so he gets the warped impression that anyone with a little common sense should be able to do it, but he's not making it! After he has used Roman numerals, Arabic figures, and algebra, you're ready to do it to him. Pick up the piece of paper and tear off each of the four corners. Even a blind man can now tell him that it has eight new corners.

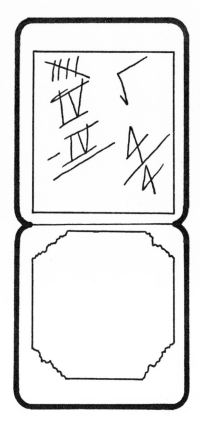

Picking Up the Change

If someone has carelessly left a few coins on the table, you can make them yours without thievery. Just get the old conversation ball rolling.

"Nobody can follow even the simplest instructions these days."

"Come on, things aren't that bad."

"Don't tell me they aren't. You're one of the smartest people around here, but I'll bet even you don't follow instructions very well."

"Of course I do."

"Well let's see. I bet you can't answer three questions with the word, oh, 'apples.' "

"You think I'm so dimwitted I can't answer 'apples' to three questions? You're on."

"Okay, it's a bet. When I ask you three questions you will answer 'apples' to all three of them. Right?"

"Right."

"Okay, what's the third day of the week?"

"Apples."

"Right. What are yellow and grow in bunches?"

"Apples."

"Right, again. Let's see . . . what would you rather have, apples or the change on this table?"

If he answers "The change," he loses and you collect the bet. On the other hand, if he answers "Apples," you pick up the money.

So Close

"Boy, did you see those Japanese wrestling matches on television? Those sumo guys are really great. Wow, they stand there with both feet planted firmly on the mat and then struggle and strain to upset the other one. One of them did a balancing trick where he almost never got knocked over. I think I figured it out. I'd like to try it with one of them. I'll bet I could do it."

"You mean you think one of those guys couldn't knock you off your feet? Even I could do that."

"Maybe one of them could, but one thing is sure, you can't. In fact, I'll bet you a buck that if you stand on one end of a dollar bill and I stand on the other end of the same bill, I can adopt a certain position and you won't be able to knock me off my end."

When you get the go-ahead from your student, place his bill on the floor in the center of a doorway (making sure the door closes from your side) and have him stand on the last two inches of his end of the bill. Now close the door and stand on your end. Once he realizes he's been had, your only problem is getting him off the bill so you can put it in your pocket.

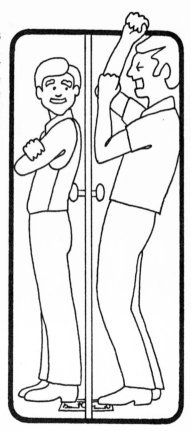

Where's the 6?

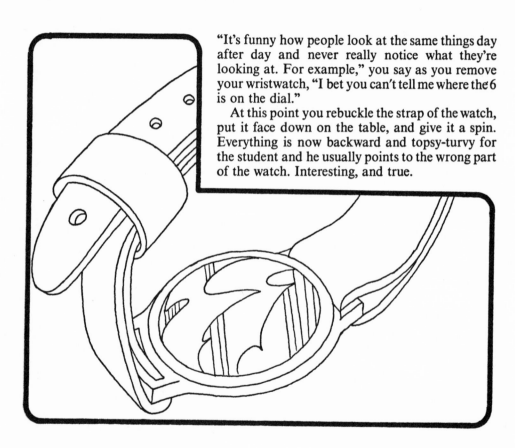

"It's funny how people look at the same things day after day and never really notice what they're looking at. For example," you say as you remove your wristwatch, "I bet you can't tell me where the 6 is on the dial."

At this point you rebuckle the strap of the watch, put it face down on the table, and give it a spin. Everything is now backward and topsy-turvy for the student and he usually points to the wrong part of the watch. Interesting, and true.

Face Cards Face Up

This is a very good bet to pull during the break in an evening's card game. You start bragging about how lucky you are, and that you seem to have a very good card sense (this is an especially good ploy if you've been a loser all evening!). Finally you get down to the bet . . .

"That's right, you get to shuffle the deck and cut it into two piles. We each take a pile and simultaneously deal cards onto the table, and I bet that you turn up a face card before I do."

When you get your packet of cards hold them face down in your left hand. As your right hand removes each card tip it slightly so you can see its face, then turn it face up on the table. This should not be done surreptitiously, but just as though you were checking to see if you were going to get "struck." However, as soon as you see a face card, deal it face down onto the table. Nine times out of ten your opponent will give a cry of triumph and turn over the card to show it is a face card. You then pick up the bet because *he* turned the card face up, not you!

A Ripoff

"I know you're clever with your hands, but here's a toughie. I've made two tears in this strip of paper and I'll bet that, by holding one end in each hand, you can't tear off both ends in one pull."

Of course he can't, so you win the bet. Remember, a chain is only as strong as its weakest link.

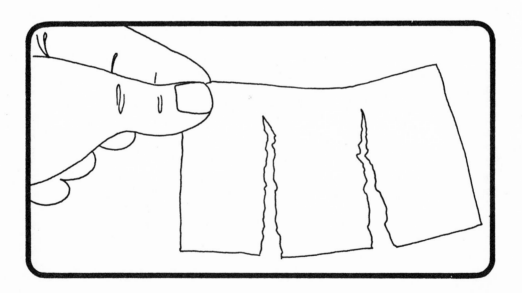

To's Too's Two's

Here is the perfect bet for you if you like to watch frustration run across people's faces. Bet them they can't write a simple eight-word sentence, in English, that you dictate. When they're ready with poised pencil and paper, say—

"There are three to's in the English language."

I had to write it incorrectly in order to give it to you, but at least now you see what the problem is. There isn't any way to write the fourth word.

However, don't make the same mistake I did. When I was dictating this chapter to my secretary, she looked up at me and said she could do it. It's always good to instill a little humility in an uppity employee so I agreed to let her try. After I said the sentence she turned her pad around and showed me—

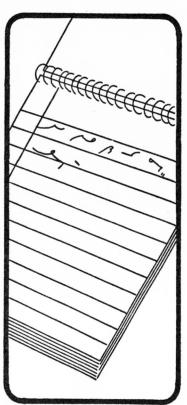

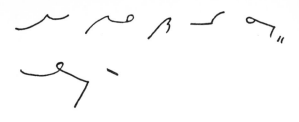

A New Word

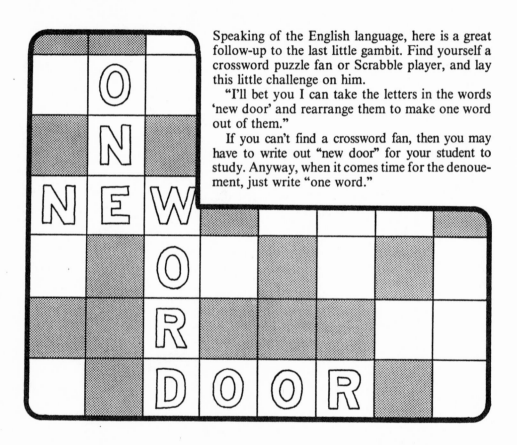

Speaking of the English language, here is a great follow-up to the last little gambit. Find yourself a crossword puzzle fan or Scrabble player, and lay this little challenge on him.

"I'll bet you I can take the letters in the words 'new door' and rearrange them to make one word out of them."

If you can't find a crossword fan, then you may have to write out "new door" for your student to study. Anyway, when it comes time for the denouement, just write "one word."

An Unusual Paragraph

Remember what I told you earlier about preparation? Well, here's a classic example. I don't know how old this chestnut is, but it never fails to catch a student off guard.

Type the following paragraph on a blank 3-by-5 inch filing card, and stick it in your wallet. The next time you want to stimulate some action, just take it out and give it to someone to read.

An Unusual Paragraph

What is particularly unusual about this paragraph? You won't find many paragraphs similar to it. In all probability you will not find out what is so unusual about it right away, but if you look at it and study it for long, it may dawn on you. If you should find out what is odd or unusual, don't say what it is until I ask you; if you can't find out, look on back of this card. Don't look at my solution until you fail to find out what is odd about it. I could throw you a hint but I won't!

On the other side of the card, write:
There is no "e" in the entire paragraph.

Knots to You

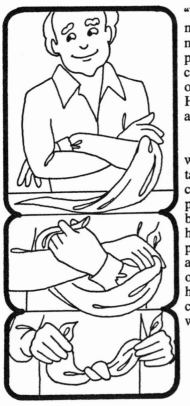

"You know, I've always been sorry that I never made Eagle Scout when I was a kid. I was great in a number of skills but just didn't have enough overall points to make Eagle. As a matter of fact, I was the champion knot-tier in all eight counties of the state of Connecticut. I won the title with something the Hartford *Courant* headlined not as a miracle but as a 'Miracle Knot.' I wonder if I could still do it."

"What did you do?"

"Oh, nothing I just tied a knot in a handkerchief without letting go of the ends." At this point you take a handkerchief out of your pocket, holding a corner in each hand as you state your unlikely accomplishment again. If he decides to try to do it himself before betting you, put the handkerchief into both his hands. However, when it comes time for you to perform drop the hanky on the table and cross your arms. Lean down and take one end of the cloth in one hand, lean in the opposite direction so the other hand can pick up the opposite corner, and then carefully unfold your arms. There is your prize-winning knot!

Connecticut champion, my eye.

Cut but Uncut

This is a cute one. You provide the string, the restaurant provides the cup, and your friend will provide the meal!

"Here, hold one end of this short string while I tie this cup to the other end. Now hold it so the cup dangles above the table. Good. I'll bet you the amount of the dinner check that I can cut that string, right in the center, but the cup won't fall. No, I won't be holding the ends in my other hand; as a matter of fact, I won't even touch the string after I cut it."

When your student tells you that he doubts your ability to defy the laws of gravity and is finally willing to make a bet on it, tie a knot in the center of the string, and then cut the loop. And I hope you do this after the dessert course; otherwise you may not get it!

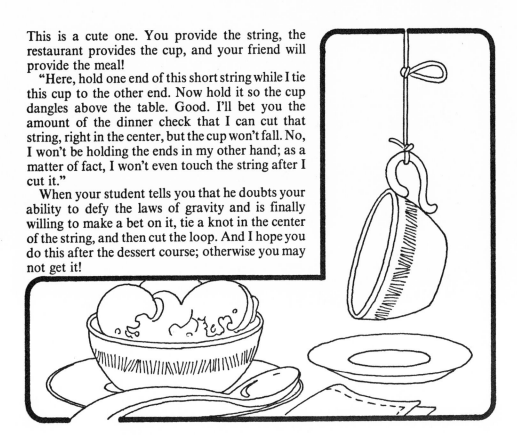

Anything I Can Do You Can Do...Well, Maybe

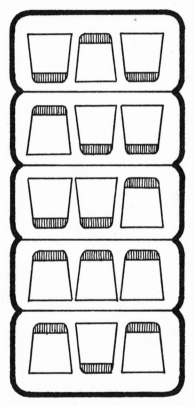

The basic principle of this little "gotcha" is that the student is unable to duplicate an apparently simple procedure. Actually, it's impossible.

"This time I'm going to give you a running chance. Here are three empty glasses on the table; the middle one opposite to the other two. I'm going to do the trick once so you know it can be done, but I'll bet you won't be able to duplicate it. Watch— one ... two ... and three. By turning two glasses at the same time, I now have them all upside down in three moves. Can you do it?"

This is a good one to finish a session with, because the student will continue to try, and try, and try, but to no avail. Start with the first glass right side up, the middle glass upside down, and the third glass right side up. Quickly turn over 1 and 2 together, then 1 and 3, and finally 1 and 2. It helps if you cross your wrists when you make the second move, to confuse the opposition, but leaving the glasses in their rightful places. Now that it's the student's turn, turn the center glass right side up. It is now impossible for him to finish in three moves with all three glasses upside down. In other words, you can *only* finish with all three glasses in the same position the middle one is in at the beginning.

An Accounting Problem

"Boy, you CPAs (computer people, math students, college grads) sure don't know much simple arithmetic. Look, here are ten coins, I'll bet you that you can't distribute the ten coins among three glasses so each glass contains an odd number of coins."

After a number of false starts the student will finally tell you it can't be done. Indeed, he'll insist that no one can do it. When you tell him that you can, he'll offer to bet right away. Merely put three coins in the first glass, two coins in the second, and five coins in the third glass.

"What's the matter," he'll say, "can't you count? You put two coins in one glass. That's not an odd number."

Now slowly pick up the third glass and nest it inside the second glass. Each glass now contains an odd number of coins.

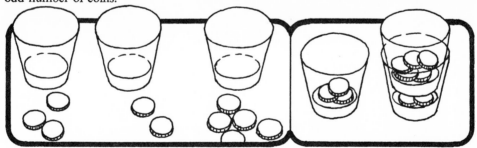

What Is It?

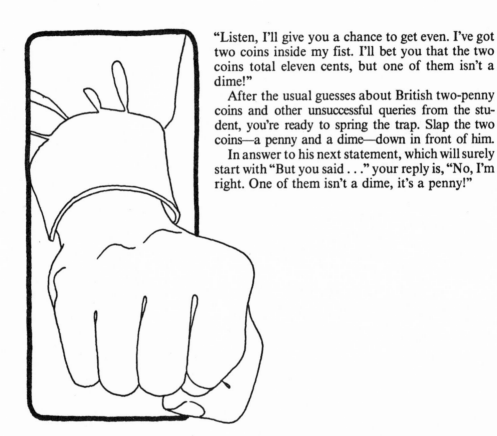

"Listen, I'll give you a chance to get even. I've got two coins inside my fist. I'll bet you that the two coins total eleven cents, but one of them isn't a dime!"

After the usual guesses about British two-penny coins and other unsuccessful queries from the student, you're ready to spring the trap. Slap the two coins—a penny and a dime—down in front of him.

In answer to his next statement, which will surely start with "But you said . . ." your reply is, "No, I'm right. One of them isn't a dime, it's a penny!"

Dry Martini

You never know where you will learn another betcha. If my memory serves me right, this particular one was shown to me by a girl who was working in our show when we played in Kansas. We used a couple of local girls to help us and she was one of them. Not only did she not drink, but you know what Kansas is like!

"With these three toothpicks I'm making a picture of a martini, and then I'm dropping a dime 'inside' the 'glass' to represent an olive. By moving only two toothpicks I bet I can remove the olive from the martini. No, I won't touch the olive!"

At the proper dramatic moment (which is when the student covers your bet) you quickly slide the center toothpick to the left, and then bring the upper right toothpick down to the lower left. As you're counting your new manna, you'll probably hear from some so-called wit that you just spilled the "martini." Look at him with disdain and inform him that you drank it first!

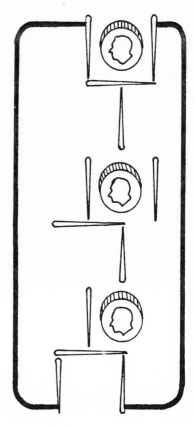

Countdown

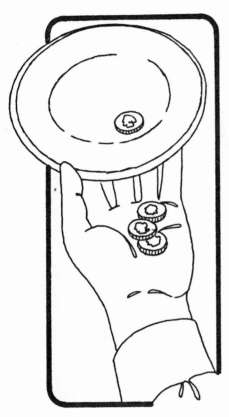

Sometimes you can lead your student down the garden path without his even knowing he's in the garden. For example, let's say you're sitting at the cafeteria lunch table and a friend is telling you about how he solved a problem no one else in the office was able to. It suddenly dawns on him that you aren't paying too much attention. Instead, you are counting quarters slowly onto a plate, one at a time. And you keep doing it over and over without a word. Finally he can't contain his curiosity and he'll ask you what's happening.

"Oh, nothing," you reply. "A simple counting problem that no one seems able to get. Maybe since you're so smart you can figure it out."

"You've come to the right man."

"Okay, I'll bet you four quarters that you can't pick them up off the table, count them one at a time onto that plate, then pick them all up again, one at a time, and still have one left on the plate."

This one usually works best if you tend to hurry and bully your student. Making him work under pressure keeps him from realizing the simplicity of the set-up. When he gives up and it's your turn, openly count the four quarters onto the plate. Now remove three of them, one at a time, and then pick up the plate with the last quarter on it.

Your Move

Sometimes you are in a perfect situation to set up this proposition because the waitress doesn't remove the empty glasses when she brings a new round of drinks. Start arranging the glasses in a row and move them around a little with a thoughtful look on your face.

"Okay, now what are you up to?"

"Well, I've moved these six glasses around until I have three full ones followed by three empty ones. Do you know that by moving only one glass you can have them alternate? That is, they'll be empty, full, empty, full, empty, full. Try it."

After a lot of shuffling around of the glasses your friend will assure you it can't be done—and he'll be right. It can't be done his way and he'll be willing to wager his new car on it. Take it easy on him, though; his sense of certainty may never be the same again.

Pick up glass number 2, pour its contents into glass number 5, and then replace it. And it's accomplished with so little effort!

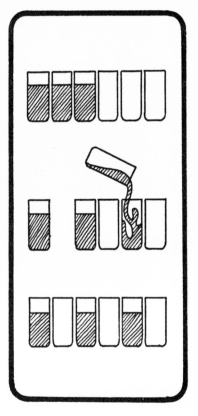

Egg of Columbus

I not only learned a lot of magic from my father, but also a lot of these betchas. Like most kids I got an allowance each week, and sometimes I even got to keep it! You see, one of his ways of teaching me a betcha so I wouldn't forget it was to bet me my allowance. I'll tell you one thing—I very quickly learned to listen to a bet very closely. But here's one where he got me twice.

We were in a restaurant and he had the waiter bring an egg from the kitchen. Showing it to me, he said he could balance it on the table. I thought about it for a while, with him smiling that knowing grin of his, but finally had to bet him to find out how to do it. He took the salt shaker and sprinkled a little pile of salt on the tablecloth. He placed the egg on the pile and firmly, but gently, settled it down. Then he very carefully blew away almost all the salt grains. Lo and behold, the egg was balanced. I lost my dollar, but I was a little wiser.

The following week—I think we were in Columbus—we were all marveling at the egg that one of the ducks had lain the night before. Then Dad tapped me on the shoulder.

"I'll bet you I can balance this egg on that crate—without using salt!"

Well, I looked around. Everyone was smiling and

waiting to see what I would do. So, there was only one thing a man of the world could do. I bet him.

He took the egg and held it with the larger end at the bottom. Very gently he hit the bottom end against the crate. Nothing happened. He hit it again and this time a little bit of the shell broke. I expected raw egg to run all over the crate, but, instead, the egg was balanced, all by itself!

Later he explained to me that the large end is the end with the little air sac for the hatching chick to use inside the egg. He hit the eggshell just hard enough to break the shell but not hard enough to rupture the air sac.

What a way to learn science!

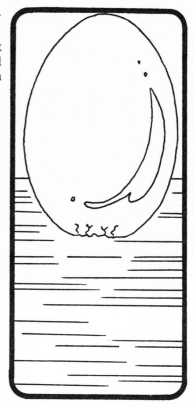

Vestward Ho!

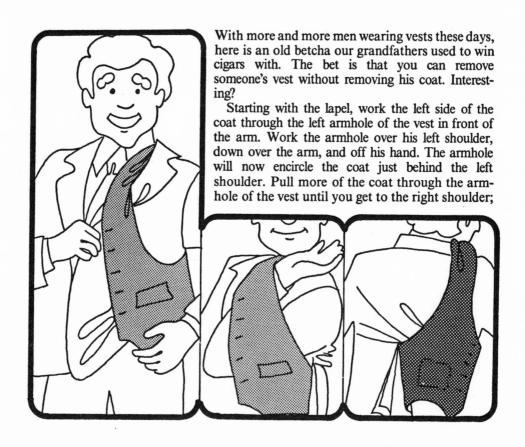

With more and more men wearing vests these days, here is an old betcha our grandfathers used to win cigars with. The bet is that you can remove someone's vest without removing his coat. Interesting?

Starting with the lapel, work the left side of the coat through the left armhole of the vest in front of the arm. Work the armhole over his left shoulder, down over the arm, and off his hand. The armhole will now encircle the coat just behind the left shoulder. Pull more of the coat through the armhole of the vest until you get to the right shoulder;

now go down the length of the sleeve, over the hand, and pull the right lapel of the coat through it. The vest is now under the coat with both armholes around the right shoulder. Work the vest down the right sleeve, on the inside, until you can reach up the sleeve from the cuff and pull the vest right out the end of the sleeve.

The two of you can now sit down and rest a bit.

Well, you've just gone through the classics. Now we'll take you out of the kindergarten into the grade school of "doing unto others before they do you!"

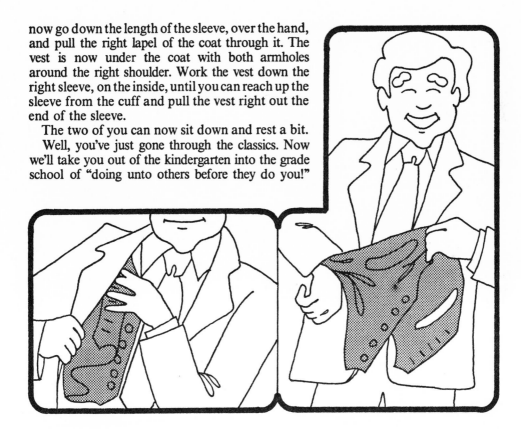

3. Scientific Principles

Contrary to lovers' theories, science is what makes the world go around—just ask any scientist. Keen of eye, steady of hand, quick of mind, dead certain of truth, scientists are without a doubt the easiest people in the world to fool. Their unquestionably sharp minds run in a straight line from point A to point B. All well and good if straight lines are what you are interested in. If, however, just a wee bit of crookedness is your game—and the fact that you're reading this book means that it is—then the scientist becomes your ideal student. All the following challenges are based on some basic fact of physics, chemistry, or general science. Most of them are classics that have been around for sixty to a hundred years, but they're still able to snap back at some unsuspecting soul who doesn't realize you can make liquid run uphill!

Sweet Betcha

You're dining out with some friends and have been idly playing with a cube of sugar during the conversation. Then, holding it up so all can see it, you say, "Did you know that although sugar will burn, it's almost impossible to light? Try it."

This should be enough to pique someone's curiosity, and he'll find that he can't get it to light at all. Now comes step number two.

"I'll bet you I can light it with one match."

When you are finally coaxed into demonstrating the impossible, you light a corner of your cube and it burns with a beautiful blue flame. What your student doesn't know is that as you picked up your cube you have put cigarette ashes on the corner you're going to light. The carbon of the ashes becomes a catalyst for the carbon in the sugar, and without it the whole thing ain't gonna work!

Cheap Compass

"I don't believe this scientific nonsense about having to know the displacement of an object before you know if it'll float. You can float anything you want, if you have the touch. Look at the Chinese—they were making compasses for a couple of hundred years before they even heard of Archimedes! They could float a piece of solid metal on water. Not a boat full of air, but solid metal. Those ancients have forgotten more than modern scientists will ever learn."

Keep talking like a heretic and eventually someone will want to correct your warped views. When the fiscal amount of how much would teach you a lesson has been determined, you can proceed to float a needle on water.

Tear out a square of tissue, place the needle on top of it, and gently drop them flat onto the surface of the water. Slowly the tissue will soak up water and finally sink. Lo and behold, there is the needle floating on the surface of the water. Score another one for the clever Chinese!

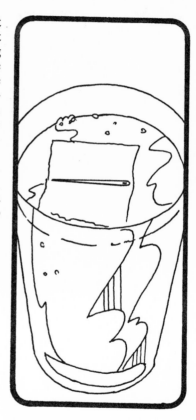

An Egg Float

"Now I've proven you can float anything if you just want to hard enough. George, bring us a raw egg. Here you are—float the egg. Come on, what do you mean it sinks? Try harder!"

People never learn and, even after the last demonstration with the needle, eventually they will coax you into showing them how. After the showing has been made worthwhile, you agree to show your skill.

Take a glass and fill it halfway with water. Now mix in salt and stir the water so the salt dissolves. Pour in more salt and do more stirring until the water won't dissolve any more salt. Put the egg in the bowl of a spoon and gently lower it onto the surface of the water. Eureka, it floats!

"You think that's good? While you were watching me stir the salt and the water, I taught this egg how to swim underwater. What do I mean? I mean that I can add more water and the egg will stay right there in the middle of the glass. Oh, yes, I can. You don't believe it? Some people never learn."

Now gently add fresh water until the glass is full and you will have an egg floating in the center of a glass, neither rising nor sinking. The brine is more dense than the egg so the egg floats on top of the salty water, but the egg is heavier than fresh water so it stays at the bottom of it.

Adrift

Is there a doctor in the house? A surgeon preferably. Someone with a lot of pride, perhaps too much, in the steadiness of his hands. Well, let's see if he is as steady as you are.

Take a glass that is almost full of water and drop a cork into it. Your student is to hold the glass in one hand and make the cork stay in the center. Unfortunately for him, the cork will keep floating to the side and stick against the side of the glass.

When it's your turn to show what a really steady hand looks like, take a second glass of water and gently pour water into the first glass. Keep pouring until the glass is not only full but the surface of the water is slightly above the rim of the glass. The cork will float to the highest point, the center of the glass. Very gently pick it up, and to everyone's surprise but yours, you've won again.

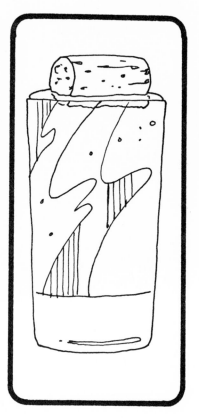

Salt and Pepper

While you're still sitting at the table, reach for the salt shaker again and this time pour a small pile in the center of the table and a larger pile about a foot away from it. Now pick up the pepper shaker and add pepper to both piles.

As you mix each pile look at your rapt spectators and say something like, "I really do have special talents. For example, I can separate salt and pepper mixed in a pile faster than anyone else. In fact, I'm so confident of my skill, you can even pick the pile I work with."

Inevitably you'll get the larger pile, but don't worry about a thing. You might even add a little extra just to show off. When the signal to begin is given, take out a comb and run it through your hair a few times. Wave it closely over the top of the pile and the little pepper flakes will literally jump out of the pile and stick to the comb. Wipe them off and repeat the process until the static electricity in the comb has removed all the pepper. Pick up the bet and tell your audience what a charge you got out of teaching them a little bit about science . . .

Hair-Raising

The next time the waitress serves the table with a glass of water, look at the floating ice cubes and start talking about how your barber said that you have the most extraordinary hair he ever saw. Not only is your hair strong, but he claimed it is also magnetic or something because it can attract and hold heavy objects.

"What's that you say, you think my hair-cutter's crazy? Well, my friend, he isn't. Prove it? Here? At the table? Okay. Supposing I were to, let's say, lift one of the cubes out of the water by using a hair from my head. That would do it, huh? Good."

As soon as it has been settled about who will pay the dinner check, start reaching for the salt shaker. Lay the center of the hair across the top of a cube and sprinkle salt on it. Wait for about a minute, and gently lift the two ends of the hair and the cube will come right out of the glass. The salt melted the surface of the ice but the cold of the cube refroze it, this time around the center of the hair.

Drop-In

This is an oldie, but maybe it's so old that everyone in your crowd has forgotten it. Slowly bend a wooden match until it breaks, but don't separate the halves. Now set the match across the mouth of a shot glass or liqueur glass, and lay a dime on top of the match. Challenge anyone to drop the dime into the glass, but without touching the match, the glass, or the dime.

When it's your turn, dip your finger into a glass of water, and then let a drop of it fall onto the break in the match. The water will swell the wood, which will make the match open up, dropping the dime into the glass.

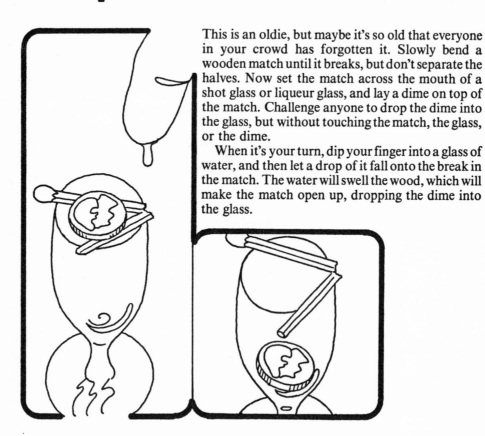

Hot Stuff

This is especially good at a picnic or outdoor barbecue, and you'll see why in a moment. Anyway, you're sitting there at the table and you comment on how hot it is. Everyone agrees. Hot enough to fry an egg on the ground maybe? Hot enough to boil water in a paper cup without leaving the table? What do they mean, certainly not? Of course it is and, for a small fee, you'll show them how to do it.

When the hullabaloo dies down you reach for a paper cup and the pitcher of punch, lemonade, water, or whatever. Pour a little more than 1/8 inch of water into the cup, which should not be a waxed cup, by the way, and then pick up a cigarette lighter. Flick on the lighter and hold it under the cup. During the oh's and ah's you just keep watching the water. And don't worry about the black on the bottom of the cup; it looks as though the paper is burning but it isn't. You see, the water is carrying the heat away from the paper, so the paper won't burn. It's just like when you put a spoon into a cup to keep it from cracking when pouring in hot coffee. Anyway, in a short while you will see the bubbles start forming and then, lo and behold, the water will boil.

A small cup of hot punch, anyone?

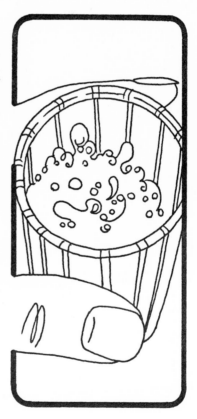

Going Up

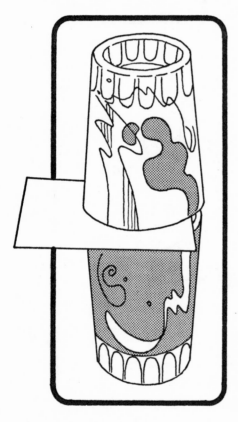

Now ask the keeper of the glasses to give you another glass, just like the one you used in Drop-In. Have one glass filled with whiskey and the other with water. Push the two glasses around on the table until they are about three inches apart and squint at them appraisingly.

"What are you doing?" someone will ask.

"Oh, nothing," you reply, "just figuring out a way to transfer the liquids in those two glasses without using another container."

"You mean the whiskey will be in that glass and the water will be over there in the other glass but you won't use a container to pour one glass out? Without using your mouth it can't be done."

"Yeah? Just watch."

Pick up the glass of water and put a business card over its mouth; holding it firmly, turn it upside down and set it on the other glass. Now slide the card until there is about 1/8 inch between the edge of the card and the inside edges of the two glasses. The water, being heavier than the whiskey, will start flowing down into the lower glass, thereby forcing the whiskey to travel up and replace the departing water in the upper glass. After a few seconds, depending on the width of the opening, the two liquids will be in the opposite glasses.

Heads Down

Here's where you get to brag about your Uncle Mike, that grand old man who dearly loved a glass of beer. The only problem was that he didn't like to have a head on it. Dear old Uncle Mike had spent years of his beer-drinking life slowly pouring the golden liquid down the side of his glass so he wouldn't get a head, until the day he met the sea captain. Never did know the name of that sea captain, but he scoffed at Uncle Mike for wasting all that valuable time pouring when he could be using it for drinking.

Well, Uncle Mike finally wormed the secret out of the old salty dog, and he went around the rest of his natural life with a smile on his face. What for, you say? Because now he knew how to put the head of his beloved beer at the bottom of the glass. Give me a clean, dry glass and I bet I can put the head at the bottom of the glass.

After you get the glass have it filled with beer, then drink some of it so the top of the head is slightly below the edge of the glass. Now take a beer mat, or the cardboard from the back of a scratch pad, and place it over the mouth of the glass. Hold the two firmly together and turn the glass upside down. Glory be, the head is now at the bottom of the glass!

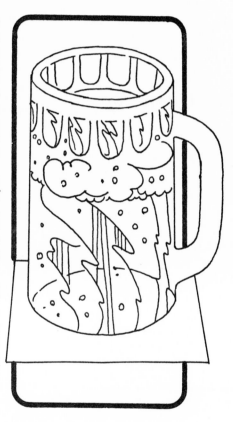

Window Wager

Have you ever watched a real carpenter at work—a man who didn't need blueprints and could make anything you described? I remember an old man in Colon, Michigan, like that. He built a couple of large tricks for the Blackstone show and taught me a couple of his own.

Anyway, I remember one time when the local banker was building his house and was driving everyone crazy with his penny-pinching. For one thing, he thought glass was too expensive and he wanted to change the big picture window in the living room. He liked the size, the eight-foot height and the nine-foot width, but it cost too much, and no one was giving him answers he liked.

Then this old carpenter stopped by one day. He listened and very slowly said, "All right, I'll put you in a window that's the same height and width, but with only half the area. That way you'll pay only half as much. You won't have to pay for a lot of cutting, either, because it'll be in one piece."

Well, the banker thought about that, couldn't figure out how to do it, but loved the idea. So the old man did it.

Never happened? Of course it did.

The next time you run into some smart carpenter just ask him and see if he's smart enough to cut the window in a diamond shape. As you can see by the illustration, it's the same, only it's half!

Looking at You

Look around and see if you can find a stranger who is wearing glasses. The challenge doesn't have to be directed at him, but basically you say you have no need for eye doctors because you can tell about a man's sight, whether he is nearsighted or farsighted or has astigmatism, just by trying on his glasses.

Actually, this is somewhat of a prevarication. As you slowly bring the glasses up to put them on, and again when you slowly take them off, you are looking through one of the lenses at some object a distance away. If the object is diminished in size it means the lens is correcting nearsightedness; if it is magnified, the lens is correcting farsightedness. Rotate the lens a little and if the object changes shape there is a correction for astigmatism. Very sneakily check the left lens as you bring the glasses up, and the right one as you take them off to hand them back. After you have returned them make your diagnosis.

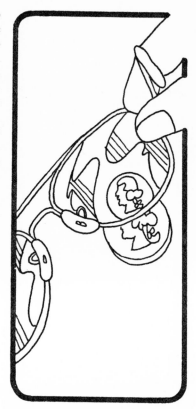

Sitting Bull's Arrow

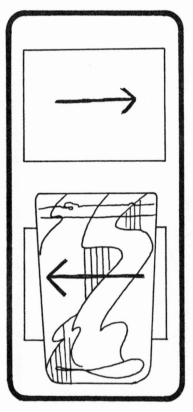

Draw a simple arrow on a piece of paper. Show it to your ever-attentive audience and challenge anyone to make the arrow go in the opposite direction, but without turning the paper around or flopping it over.

The answer is to put the drawing behind a straight-sided glass full of liquid. The liquid will act as a lens and will optically reverse the direction of the arrow.

Notice especially how wide open the terms are on this plot. No matter what questions they come up with, you can counter them. There are no loopholes in the truth . . . in this one, at least!

4. Physical Accomplishments
Real and Fake

You must have at least one of them within the circle of your acquaintances: the athlete (or ex-athlete) or Monday-morning quarterback who is more concerned whether Ohio will meet California than whether the sun will come up tomorrow. He's the kind of guy who's proving his masculinity at every opportunity.

Well, now here's your chance to let him prove it. The nicest thing about these types is that you rarely need to lay a trap for them. They're just walking around waiting for someone to make them live up to their boasts.

The following propositions make up a kind of civilian obstacle course for these fellows. Some of these little beauties can be done, if you know how, and others are simply impossible. So that you won't get caught off guard if the physical-culture student turns and tries to finagle you into doing it, I've noted the impossible ones.

Cash Reflex
(Impossible)

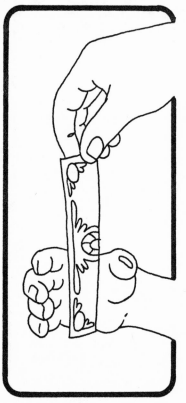

"Everyone knows that you're in good physical condition and your reflexes are probably extra sharp, Charlie. Well, let's find out just how sharp they are."

Put a lengthwise crease in a fairly new bill and hold it by one end in a vertical position in your right hand. Hold the thumb and index finger of your left hand about an inch apart and place them halfway between the portrait and the bottom end of the bill.

Drop the bill and catch it with your left hand. Do it again so your student can see how easily you do it, and then ask him to do the same. He places his finger and thumb on either side of the bill where you had yours.

Tell him that you're going to drop the bill and if he catches it he can have it.

Good luck, Charlie!

Deep Dollar Bend
(Impossible)

When the conversation becomes monopolized about how staying in perfect physical shape is the one and only way to live, that's the time to separate the doers from the talkers.

Ask your student if he can touch his toes without bending his knees. When he says yes, get a demonstration, and no matter how perfectly he does it, tell him you saw those knees bend. You, however, have a fair test which will make absolutely sure that his knees stay ruler straight. Is he game? Of course he is, and he's lost the game besides.

Put him with his heels and back against a wall, and then put a dollar bill on the floor just in front of his toes. Tell him that if he can reach down, without bending his knees, and pick up the dollar, it's his. It won't be.

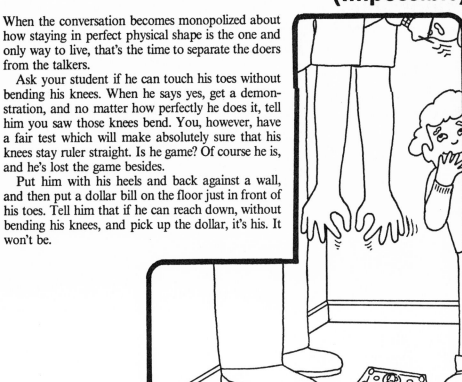

A Simple Tear
(Impossible)

Remember the beer can crushers in the days before aluminum cans, and the guy who kept bragging how he could tear his hometown telephone book in half? The next time your ears are being bombarded by this bombast, find out if the boaster can tear a sheet of newspaper in half.

"You really have strong hands, huh? How many pages in that phone book? Five hundred? I've heard a lot of guys make that boast but I've never seen one who was half as strong as he claimed. Let's just see how good you really are. I tell you what—I bet you can't tear a page of a newspaper in half, put the two halves together, tear it again, put the halves together, and tear it again—I bet you can't tear it, say, nine times."

By now, if he hasn't torn you in half for the way you're ribbing him, he's ready for the bet. You can start him with a double-page spread of paper, if you wish, or, if you want to hedge the possibilities a little, a single page. In either case, he won't get past the eighth tear. After that exertion he has 256 layers of 2-inch-square paper and there's no way he can keep them together to tear . . . even if he had the strength!

Then Tear This

The next time your newspaper-tearing unchampion forgets himself and starts making noises again about his strength, here's a perfect follow-up. Casually take a couple of dinner napkins (paper, of course), open them out flat, and then twist each one individually into a hard rope shape. Challenge the world's strongest barfly to tear one of these little napkins in half. If he tries he'll fail, but if about this time he gets a hazy recollection of being had by you once before, he'll probably challenge you to do it first. Which you proceed to do. Now it's really up to him, but he's out of it and just doesn't know it.

Also what he doesn't know is that just before you reach for the twisted napkin, you secretly wet the tips of both thumbs. When you pick up the napkin with your fingers, you touch your thumbtips to the center of the napkin. The moisture will soak into the paper and weaken it just enough so you're able to do your half of the bargain.

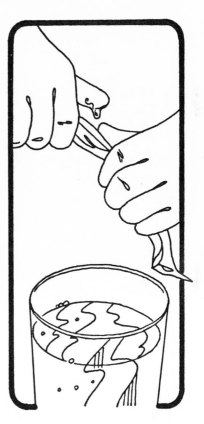

Strong Fingers

Sometimes he likes to put his physical strength on a personal basis, and when he does here's a little demonstration that should make him think twice about making it too personal.

Have the physical specimen close each fist and place one on top of the other. You, using only the index finger of each hand and just tapping his fists, easily separate his hands. When you exchange positions, however, he finds that he simply can't knock your fists apart.

When you hit his fists with your fingers, aim for his knuckles and strike them away from each other. Now when you close your own fists and put them together, secretly slide your lower thumb up into your other fist. Your hands are now as immovable as two boulders.

Water Guard

Here's the perfect method for proving that the brain is mightier than the muscle. Put a glass of your favorite liquid in your right hand and state that your student isn't strong enough to prevent you from taking even one drink.

When he's ready, have him grasp your wrist firmly with both his hands. Perhaps he'd like to brace his feet on the floor in some way too. After all, you don't want to take unfair advantage. For a little added drama let someone count to three so you will both be prepared for the mighty effort.

When the moment comes simply reach over with your left hand, take the glass, and down a refreshing swig. Maybe you'd better offer him one, too—he still has your arm in his possession!

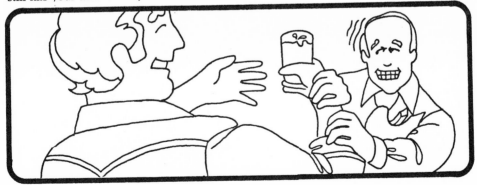

Push-of-War
(Impossible)

Here's face-to-face combat that will leave your adversary huffing and puffing with a very red face, while you're still calm and cool.

Find a broom and have the student hold it horizontally, with his hands slightly farther apart than his shoulders. You can force your student to grasp the broom in this manner, by holding your hands so that your fists are opposite the student's shoulders and his hands are on the outside of yours. You close each of your hands into a fist with the thumb pointing straight up and then put them against the broom, about six inches on each side of the center. When you're ready, he is to try and knock you off balance by pushing the broom. However, you easily resist his strongest efforts.

How? When he begins pushing against your thumbs, simply exert an upward pressure with your fists. Each of his arms is being directed slightly outward, and his remaining strength is being pushed so all his force is directed in three directions at once and easily resisted.

Three-to-One
(Impossible)

When your student finally asks for some help to overcome your obvious superiority, let him get two of his friends to help on his end of the broom.

"With three of you on one end and me all alone on the other, I bet I can keep you from pushing my end into a six-inch circle on the floor. That's right, the three of you against poor, weak, little old me."

They hold the broom with the straws pointing toward the ceiling and with their hands about a third of the length of the handle below the straws. The target circle is made on the floor, and they start with the end of the broom handle about 18 inches above it. You place the palm of your open hand against the handle, at the end, and tell them to try to put the end of the handle into the target.

Their strenuous efforts and obvious failures are enough to warrant an entertainment tax on the bystanders. All you do is simply push the end of the handle sideways, keeping it outside the circle.

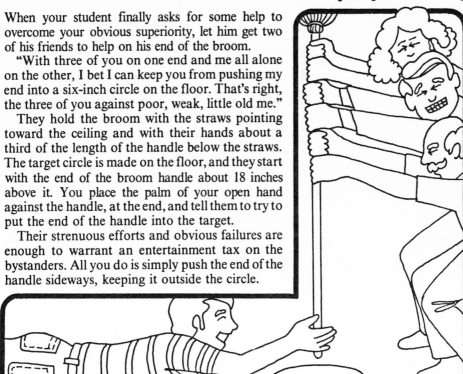

Five-Finger Lift

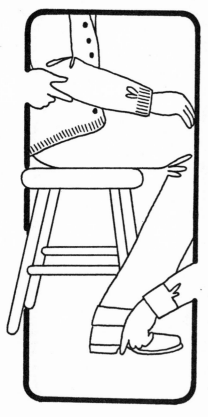

This eye-opening stunt very easily demonstrates that any man can be a pushover under the right circumstances, especially just after he's bragged about how big a man he is. Tell him, "I bet you're not that heavy. As a matter of fact, I bet I can lift you with just five fingers." Watch the slow smile of delight come over his face as he thinks of you trying to lift great big him. Is he in for a surprise!

Have the student sit in an armless chair with his arms crossed. You and four friends are now easily going to lift him out of the chair using just one finger each.

The first person puts a forefinger under the instep of the left shoe, and the second person does the same with the right shoe. The third person hooks his finger around the bone just in front of the student's left elbow, while someone else takes the same position at his right elbow. Finally, you put your index finger crosswise under his chin so you support both sides of the jawbone. As you count to three the person in the chair is to lock his joints so he becomes a solid object, but without stiffening his muscles. He is merely to prevent his knees and other body hinges from bending. At the same time you and the other four are taking a deep breath. On the count of three you all hold your breath and lift. Up comes your student.

Dressing It Up

Here's a beautiful proposition the next time someone happens to drop, spill, or knock over something.

"I know you're a little uncoordinated, but I didn't know you were that bad. Do they really let you out of the house in the morning? Who puts your clothes on you? Why, I'll bet you can hardly button your own shirt. As a matter of fact, I bet you can't button up your shirt in less than ten seconds!"

Have your backward student pull out his shirt and unbutton the front. Now challenge him to button up his shirt in less than ten seconds from the time you say "go." He will give it a valiant effort and might even come close to beating the time limit. But when he's all done, point out that he buttoned it down, not up!

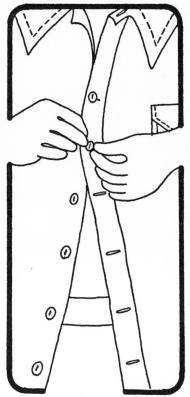

5. Small Cons

We have, traditionally, been brought up to help the underdog, to uplift the downtrodden, and aid weaker individuals. Why this bit of social observation? It's so the next time you wonder whether it's ethical to bet someone on a proposition when you alone know the real answer, just remember the story of the two kids playing rummy. Their uncle noticed that the girl was memorizing and stacking the cards every chance she got. He brought this to the attention of her brother, who was unconcerned about the whole thing. "So what?" he said. "It's her deal!"

Toss-Up

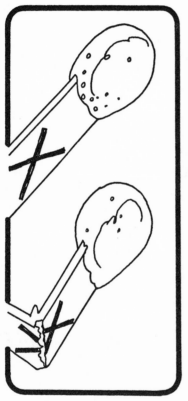

"Tell you what, Charlie," you say one evening. "You've been so generous buying the drinks that I insist you let me have a chance to do the next round. Here, I'll take this paper match and put an X on this side, and if that side is up when the match lands on the bar, I'll buy the next round. Not only that, but I'll put another X on the other side—see it?—and if that X shows when the match lands I'll still buy the round. Okay, here we go."

The only thing is, when you drop your hand to toss the match into the air your thumb bends the match in half. The next time Charlie sees the match it's on its side on the bar. "Gee, Charlie, I guess you'll have to buy the next round, too."

Date Guessing

Study the change when a waitress puts it on the table and soon your friends will ask what you are looking for. Well, you remark, you read in the newspaper a few months ago that a rare penny had recently sold for $500, so you have been studying coins for the last few months and are really becoming quite knowledgeable. As a matter of fact, you insist that you can tell a lot about coins because of all the study you've given them. For example, if someone will put a quarter face down in front of you, you will name the date it was minted. You are so sure of your skill that you will give the student a dime for every quarter that you guess wrong.

Have a number of dimes ready because there is going to be some fast shuffling in a few moments. After all the quarters have been put face down in front of you stare intently at the first one. Name a date and turn the coin over. If you're right, great! If you're wrong, put down a dime on the table and pull the quarter toward you out of the line. Continue on down the row of quarters until you've finished. Then go back and pick up each quarter which was a wrong guess and put it in your pocket. Didn't you say you'd give him a dime for every quarter you guessed wrong?

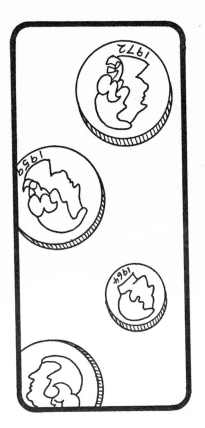

Geography

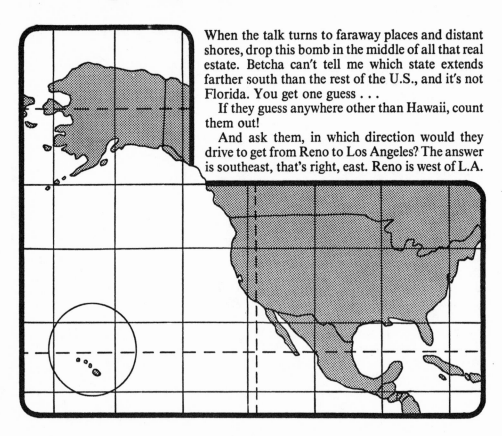

When the talk turns to faraway places and distant shores, drop this bomb in the middle of all that real estate. Betcha can't tell me which state extends farther south than the rest of the U.S., and it's not Florida. You get one guess . . .

If they guess anywhere other than Hawaii, count them out!

And ask them, in which direction would they drive to get from Reno to Los Angeles? The answer is southeast, that's right, east. Reno is west of L.A.

A Body of Land

"All right," you say to that person who can tell you the capital of all fifty states, "if you know so much about people and places, tell me where to find the following places:

> Island of Reil
> McBurney's Point
> Tunnel of Corti

Then spread a map of the world in front of him and tell him that within the nearest five hundred miles you'll consider that he hit the mark.

What do you think he'll do when you tell him that they're all parts of the body? McBurney's Point is the site of local tenderness in diagnosing appendicitis, the Tunnel of Corti is located in the ear passage, and the Island of Reil is in the central lobe of your cerebrum.

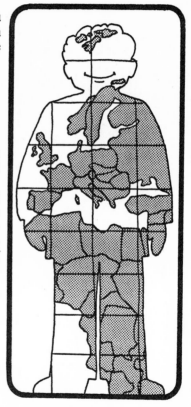

Body Geography

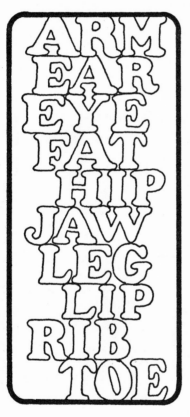

"Speaking of parts of the body," you say after the last bet, "let's see how many you know. I'll bet you that in one minute you can't name ten parts of the body that are spelled with only three letters."

Unless you've picked out a doctor traveling incognito, they're in trouble. And don't let them get a running start to ten with any halfway answers, like "Five toes and one eye make six." That's a very obvious and flippant way of trying to get around a straightforward and serious bet.

Oh, by the way, the ten parts of the body are: arm, ear, eye, fat, hip, jaw, leg, lip, rib, toe.

Heart Control

The next time the subject turns to medicine or the mysterious Indian fakirs, use this very startling demonstration to elevate your stature among your friends. Bet them that you, by using just your mental powers, can control your pulse. In other words, you can slow it down just by thinking about it. Have someone find the pulse in your wrist, and as they count out the heartbeat you close your eyes and start breathing very slowly. Surprisingly, your pulse will get slower and slower, and, if you really want to surprise them, stop it altogether. Slowly, the pulse comes back and gets stronger until it is back to normal.

How? Very simple. Just before you proposed the stunt, you sneaked a short length of pencil, a balled-up handkerchief, or small rubber ball under your armpit. Then, as they are taking your pulse, you slowly press your arm against your temporary tourniquet to cut off the flow of blood to the artery in your wrist. By releasing the pressure, you restore the beat to the pulse.

Money Auction

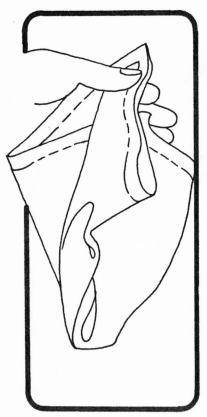

This one has to be done very slowly and deliberately so your student can see that you absolutely aren't pulling any sleight-of-hand on him. Drop a half-dollar into an empty handkerchief and have him drop 50 cents in coins in with it. Gather up the four corners like a bag and shake it a couple of times so he can hear the money rattle.

"Do you hear the coins? They're clinking, so all of them must be in there, right? All right, will you give me 75 cents for the dollar inside?"

Shake the bag again just as you say this. Some of them bite immediately, others take a few seconds to think it over. In any case, when he gives you the 75 cents, put it in your pocket, thank him, and smile a lot. After all, he just paid 25 cents for his own half-dollar!

Liar's Poker Scam

Ask your student if he has a dollar bill in his pocket or wallet, then have him bring it out, but face down so you can't see the serial number. Gaze into space for a moment and then bet him a dollar for every one of his dollar bills.

What's the bet? That each of his serial numbers has either a 7 or a 3 in it. If he hesitates, change one of the digits to a different one. In any case, the odds are 5-to-1 in your favor, so don't forget to ask for at least even money. But, in any case, you can use any two digits.

My Brand

If you ever catch a smoker eulogizing his pet brand of cigarette you might try getting him to put his money where his taste is. Challenge the smoker to identify his brand of cigarette while he's blindfolded, and bet he can't pick it out of four cigarettes.

When he's blindfolded give him his brand first, as that is when he'll least expect it. The second is a different brand, and the third one is the same as the second, but unlighted. The fourth one is another brand. Nine times out of ten the student will pick the third cigarette, the unlighted one, as his brand because of its "mildness." Enough said!

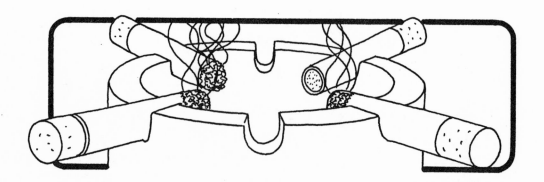

30 Full Count

For a good many years toothpicks have been used for various puzzles and brainteasers. Here's a game to determine who should pay the check, or other expenses . . .

Make a pile of 30 toothpicks and explain that the two of you will alternately remove from 1 to 6 at a time from the pile, and the player to take the last one is the winner. What you don't explain to him is that you are going to mentally keep a running total of all the toothpicks removed, and that you will make your moves equal the totals of 9, 16, and 23. When you make those moves he can't win, and that's why you don't tell him!

Let's play a game so you can follow the procedure. Suppose he starts by taking out 4. To make a running total of 9 removed, you take away 5. Now he picks up 3, making the total 12, so you take out 4 to get to 16, your second key number. Maybe now he takes only 2, so grab 5 to bring the total to 23. Now he can't win, because no matter how many he takes you'll get the last one, the winning one.

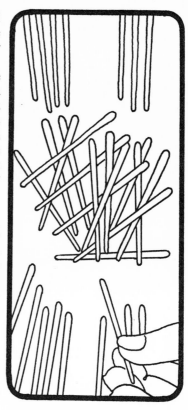

31

Once again, a very simple game to grasp. Unfortunately for the student, he finds it very difficult to win. A single die is used; the first player rolls it to come up with the first number. The second player must turn up one of the four sides, adding its number to the first one. The players alternate turning up the sides and adding the numbers until one player—the winner—turns up the final number to make a total of 31.

You need to learn a number of combinations, so memorize this little table:

Use any digit to make a total of 4
Use a 3 or 4 to make a total of 1, 5, or 9
Use a 2 or 5 to make a total of 8

These mean that on your turn you can turn up any side to make a total that when the two digits are

added together they make 4 (13 or 22, in other words). Or, if you turn up the 3 or the 4, then the two digits should total 1 (10), 5 (14 or 23), or 9 (18 or 27). Or, if the 2 or 5 are used then the digits should total 8 (17 or 26).

For example, let's say your student rolls a 3 to start the game. You turn up the 1 to bring the total to 4 (rule number 1). He turns over the 5 to make a 9, and you follow up with the 4 to make it 13 (rule number 2). A 6 is turned up, and then you bring the total to 22 with the 3. The total is brought to 27 by his using the 5, and you win by adding the 4 to make 31!

In some small-con circles this game is known as "the tat," but should rightfully be called "Fort Knox"!

Four-Five-Six

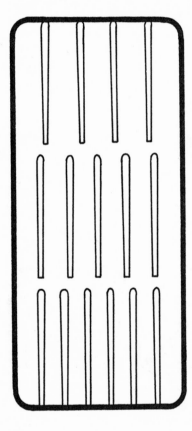

This game, you can truthfully explain to your student, is as simple as checkers to learn but as intricate as chess to play. You lay out three rows of toothpicks with four in the first row, five in the second, and six in the third. You and the student will take turns and on each turn you remove any number of toothpicks from any one row, from one toothpick to the entire row. The person taking the last toothpick is the loser. Either player can start and there isn't any discernible pattern to your play, even though you win a majority of the time.

If you have the first move you can assure your winning by removing just one from any row. Regardless of who starts, you make your moves so that your opponent is faced with the three rows making up one of the following patterns:

1 - 4 - 5   1 - 2 - 3   1 - 1 - 1

or, two rows of equal numbers.

If you remove toothpicks each time to leave one of these patterns he will be forced to take the last one. For example, let's say he's looking at 1-1-1, and then takes the one in the first row. You take the one on the second row, which leaves him the losing one in row number three.

To give a series of games a look of spontaneity, sometimes lay the toothpicks out in rows of three, five, and seven.

6. Moans and Groans
Run for Your Life!

Sometimes when you and your friends are in a certain frame of mind, feeling tolerant of the world's worst pun or lousiest joke, you'll be right on target with the following propositions. Now, just reading one of these "sillies" is terribly misleading. When you know the answer it sounds so obvious to you when you say it that it's hard to believe anyone could be fooled. But, as we have already proved, "there's one born every minute," and when you do it and the student sees it for the first time, there'll be a good surprise and reaction. It's just like telling a joke; you know the punch line that's coming, but they don't. And you laughed when you heard it for the first time, didn't you?

Use these very sparingly. I have paired some of these together because the second one works very differently from the first one, and you should catch your student a second time. But never do three on the same occasion. Also, you'd better finish each one while on your feet because the atmosphere may suddenly change when you get to the punch line, and you should remember that it's always harder for them to hit a moving target.

Magic

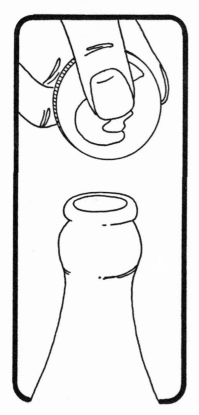

Quite often there is someone in the crowd who knows a card trick or two, and gives everyone the chance to say how much they enjoy magic. Needless to say, this is an excellent opportunity to let everyone know that you, too, have learned a trick. It took quite a while, you explain, but you finally persuaded the magician to show you how, and now you can do the impossible feat of putting a half-dollar into a pop bottle.

If most of them know you, there will probably be a couple of impolite chuckles and one derisive snort. At this show of lack of respect, you get indignant and demand the chance to prove your claim; in fact, you are willing to "put a little down on it," as they say in some circles.

After it has all been put down and an empty pop bottle provided for you, proceed to search your pockets for the money that is to make its entrance into the bottle. Remove a dollar bill from your pocket, tear it neatly in half, and after rolling one half, push it into the bottle. A *fait accompli*, as the French magicians say!

Constitutional Requirements

This is the perfect ploy when the conversation finally gets around to politics and various "expert" views are being aired. Ask the group to get down to basics and answer what should be a simple question for any American. What are the four requirements for becoming President of the United States?

The person must be at least thirty-five years of age, must be born a United States citizen, must have lived in the United States for at least fourteen years, and—this is the one they almost never get—must be elected!

FOR PRESIDENT
   G. Washington . . . . ☐
   A. Lincoln . . . . ☐
   _____ . . . . ☒

Currency Presidency

It's amazing how few people really take notice of the everyday things around them. For example, if Washington is on a one-dollar bill, and Abraham Lincoln is on a five-dollar bill, which President is on a ten-dollar bill?

Until you tell them, they probably won't remember that Alexander Hamilton wasn't ever President!

Z, Y, X, W, V...

Someone at a party eventually brings up the subject of tongue-twisters, probably to see if they're all properly oiled. But, when they do, challenge anyone to a real duel of speech. Bet them that you can say the alphabet backward faster than they can.

When you're accepted with your abecedarian (look it up!) contest, face your opponent and ask for someone to give the starting signal. As soon as it is given, turn your back on your adversary and recite the alphabet in the normal manner (A, B, C, D, etc.). You did promise to recite it backward, didn't you? You just didn't say to whom!

Cool Heat

This is good only for people who haven't had more than two drinks. More than two doesn't make them dangerous, they will just have slower comprehension and you may be stuck all night explaining what you mean.

Find yourself the perfect student, under the circumstances, and say to his or her innocent and unsuspecting face, "I challenge you to say light without heat three times real fast." When they have finished you repeat, "But I challenged you to say light without heat, three times." And this can go on interminably, which is a rather long time, until they wake up to the fact that you just want them to say the one word, "light."

Which Color?

This is a perfect dodge to use on those who are always right, even while they're making a mistake. If you can't find one of those, then use it on the student you got with the last betcha.

"I bet I can make you say 'purple.'"

"Oh, no, you can't!"

"All right, what color are your eyes?"

"Blue."

"What color are your socks?"

"Black."

"See, I told you I'd make you say 'black.'"

"You said 'purple,' not 'black' so I win the . . ."

Now you know why I call the chapter, "Moans and Groans!"

What's Wrong?

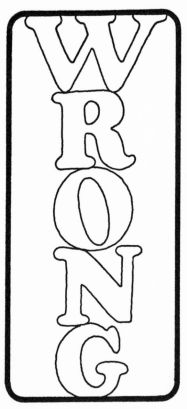

If you encounter a student of etymology, or even a crossword puzzle fan, you can hold your next lesson. It goes something like this.

"I'll bet you whatever you feel your pride is worth that, without using a pencil and paper, you can't spell three common English words in one try each."

"Oh, go on, sure I can!"

"Okay, spell 'receive.'"

"R-e-c-e-i-v-e."

"Believe."

"B-e-l-i-e-v-e."

"Wrong."

"What? B-e-l-i-e-v-e, believe."

"Wrong."

How many times do you think you will have to tell them the word before they spell w-r-o-n-g?

Wrong Hypnotism

If the subject ever gets around to hypnotism (and what's to keep you from steering it a little?), or you've just done the previous betcha, try this little challenge on one of the girls. I say a girl because they like to use their eyes more. Bet her whatever you can arrange that you can make her close her eyes and then open them again. Right away she is way ahead of you and knows that she won't open them when you ask her to, so you'll get a firm affirmative.

"Okay, close your eyes."

She does so.

"No, not that way!" If she doesn't open them again immediately to see what you mean, then she must have fallen asleep . . .

Left vs. Right

For a person who is fairly well coordinated, this is a perfect sneaky. Bet them that you can put something, not heavy, in their left hand that they can't hold in their right hand.

When the challenge has been properly financed and the student is ready to learn his lesson, simply cup his right elbow in his left hand. End of lesson.

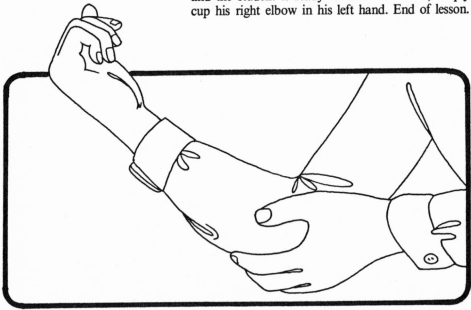

Mental Effort

Psychicism and the occult are all the rage now and probably will be for a number of years to come. When someone shows a bit of erudition and awe for the psychic world, give him a chance to stumble a little. Tell him you can turn him into a telepath, a mind reader, if you will, in a very simple manner. He will express great interest and that's when you bait the trap.

Write something on a piece of paper without letting anyone see what it says. Ask the occultic student, "Do you know what I wrote?" Since you didn't show it, naturally the answer is "no."

Then you can show the paper with a flourish and let everyone read the large NO scrawled in your personal handwriting. Another psychic success!

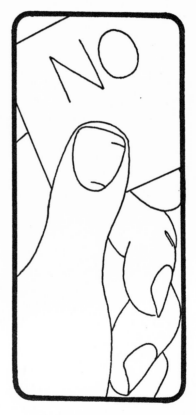

All Wet

For the last dare of the evening, bet someone they can't pour their last drink down their neck without getting their shirt wet. Usually you will be challenged to do it first, which you agree to do. Pick up the glass and drink it!

Groan!

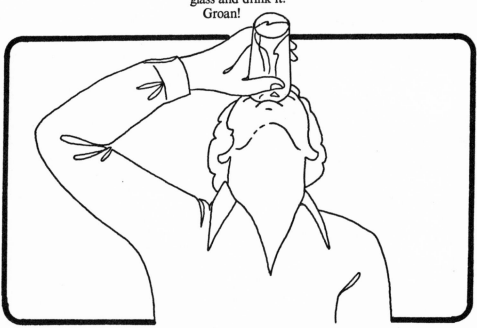

7. Practice Makes Adequate

Things to Learn to Do

The collection of ploys has gimmicks within the gimmicks. Even when you show the student how to accomplish the maneuver, quite often he still can't. That's because of a little extra practice you've put in. Not so much that it's noticeable, but enough to master the skill. They're something like that old test of patting your head with your right hand while you're rubbing your stomach with your left. If you're lucky enough to meet a person who's proud of his ability to accomplish that stunt, you'll have found your perfect student for these ploys.

One thing, there is a trick to each one of these little traps, so don't expect to do it the first time you try it. Only practice will make you an adequate teacher, so keep trying. And only a casual "anyone can do this, why can't you" air will make them truly effective, so keep practicing.

Speaking of practice, we finish this chapter with four set-ups that will definitely take a little time to learn. But they are worth every second you spend with them.

Around and Around

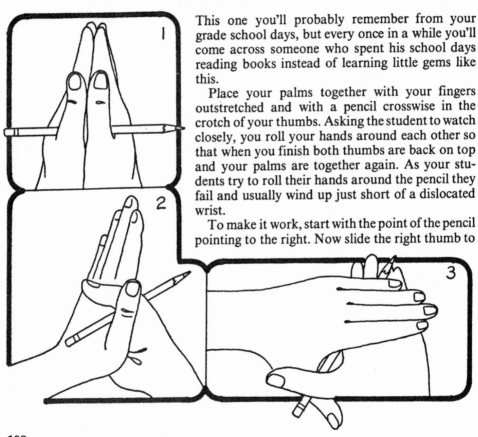

This one you'll probably remember from your grade school days, but every once in a while you'll come across someone who spent his school days reading books instead of learning little gems like this.

Place your palms together with your fingers outstretched and with a pencil crosswise in the crotch of your thumbs. Asking the student to watch closely, you roll your hands around each other so that when you finish both thumbs are back on top and your palms are together again. As your students try to roll their hands around the pencil they fail and usually wind up just short of a dislocated wrist.

To make it work, start with the point of the pencil pointing to the right. Now slide the right thumb to the left so it goes in between the knuckle of the index finger and thumb of the left hand. Keep your palms together, sliding the fingers of the left hand up toward the ceiling, as you rotate each thumb around the other. Let the point of the pencil slide under the left fingers as your palms rotate around the pencil. You should wind up with both thumbs below the pencil and both palms facing the floor.

To continue, use the same thumb-around-thumb action, continuing to rotate the palms around the pencil, letting the eraser end slide up between the two palms and past the left fingers, and you should finish back in the original position. Now hand the pencil to someone else so you can watch the fun . . .

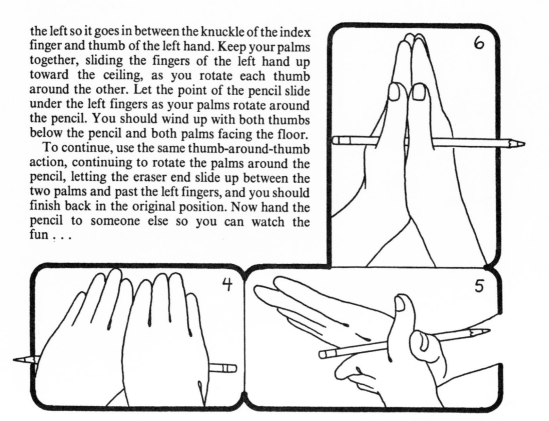

Points Up!

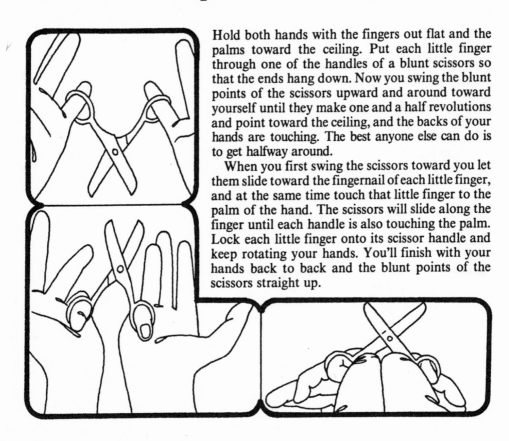

Hold both hands with the fingers out flat and the palms toward the ceiling. Put each little finger through one of the handles of a blunt scissors so that the ends hang down. Now you swing the blunt points of the scissors upward and around toward yourself until they make one and a half revolutions and point toward the ceiling, and the backs of your hands are touching. The best anyone else can do is to get halfway around.

When you first swing the scissors toward you let them slide toward the fingernail of each little finger, and at the same time touch that little finger to the palm of the hand. The scissors will slide along the finger until each handle is also touching the palm. Lock each little finger onto its scissor handle and keep rotating your hands. You'll finish with your hands back to back and the blunt points of the scissors straight up.

Up Flip

Have your student hold his arm in front of himself with the hand out flat, the fingers together and flat, and his palm facing the floor. Put a nickel or quarter on his knuckles and a second one near the wrist. Ask him to flip the two coins into the air and catch them one at a time before they hit the floor. He'll do so, and then wonder what was so hard about that. Not a thing, you reply, as you now put three coins on the back of his hand, one each on the wrist, knuckles, and fingertips. On the first toss he'll find he's in deep water, because he may hit the third coin, but he has a hard time actually catching it.

The secret to catching all three coins one at a time is to bend your knees and dip your body as the coins fall. When you do this you have practically no trouble at all. Actually, you've practiced ahead of time, so the knack has become a natural action for you.

And if you want to make absolutely sure no one can match you, practice with four coins!

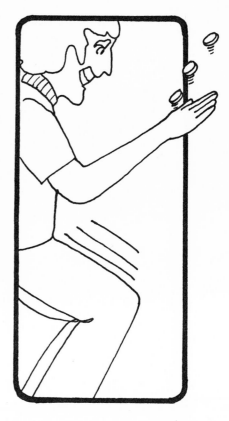

Manual Elevator

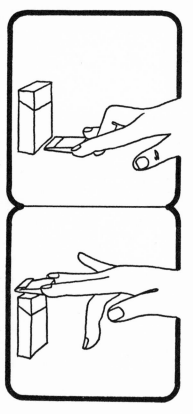

You stand a pack of cigarettes on end, place a book of matches about 1/8 inch away from the pack, with the striking strip closest to the cigarettes, and then put your middle finger on the table about 1/8 inch away from the book of matches. Keeping the tip of your middle finger firmly on the table, your first and ring fingers reach forward together, pick up the book of matches, and lift it up to the top of the cigarette pack. The challenge is for anyone within the sound of your voice to duplicate the feat.

They'll try, and try and try and try. In fact, I've had students come back to me the following day with a very sore arm because they spent hours trying to do this one simple little feat. However, physiology is against them. The secret is when you lift the matchbook off the table. You must not lift your hand until your first and ring fingers have brought the book up as high as they can. Now you move your hand up off the table and deposit the matches on top of the pack. If you move your hand too soon the muscles of your fingers will be too weak to furnish the necessary leverage.

Breakthrough

Here's an exploit tailor-made for breakfast with the gang. Carefully scoop a soft or hard-boiled egg out of half its shell. Put the shell upside down over the blade of an upright tableknife with the handle of the knife about three inches above the table. Bring the knife down, and when it hits the table its tip will poke up through the egg shell. When others try the same thing they just bounce the shell off the knife.

"Bounce" is the key word. Actually you don't hit the table with the knife handle; in reality, you let the knife drop through your fingers so that it hits the table. It will give a little bounce and that bounce will make the point pierce the shell. Simple... when you know how!

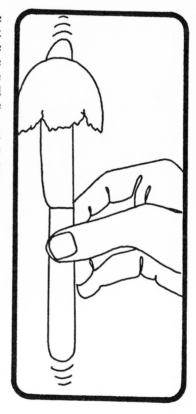

Drop It

Line up three dice and pick them up between your index finger and thumb. Snap the fingers of your other hand, and at that instant the center die drops out of your fingers without disturbing the other two. Toss the dice to someone else if they think they can do it. Remarkable how easy it looks, and how difficult it is.

A little secret knowledge is always a good ally. As you are picking up the three dice, give them a hard squeeze. When you're ready to drop the center die just slightly separate your finger and thumb. The two outside dice will stick to your skin and the middle one will fall free. Hurray for Newton and our side! And practice.

One, Two

When your audience has given up on the last bit of juggling with the dice, try this one. Wrap your middle finger and thumb around a glass and hold a die between them. You may have to experiment until you find a glass small enough to let you do this. Now stack a second die on top of the first one. Give a little toss and catch the second die in the glass. Repeat the procedure and catch the other die in the glass. The peculiar thing is that every time someone else tries it he may get the second die into the glass, but loses the first one at the same time.

Maybe what the student didn't notice is that you really don't toss the second die up into the air. Actually, you let go of the die and then drop the glass under it so that it falls into the tumbler with the first die. A small difference, but we learn to cherish such little differences . . .

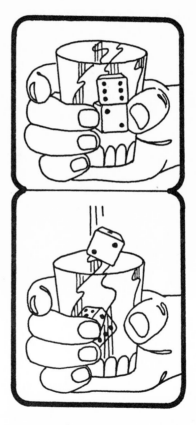

Now Smoke It

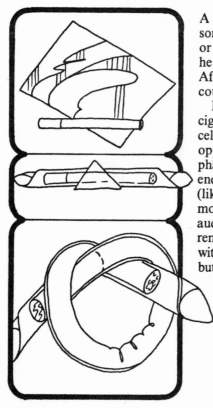

A perfect time to present this problem is when someone has just taken out either the first cigarette or the very last cigarette from his pack. Ask him if he can tie a knot in the cigarette without breaking it. After he tries it he'll say it can't be done. But, of course, you can do it!

Reach over and remove the cellophane from the cigarette package. Roll the cigarette lightly in the cellophane, but from one corner diagonally to the opposite corner. This will give you a long cellophane tail at each end of the cigarette. Take the two ends of the roll and gently tie an overhand knot (like when you start to tie your shoes in the morning) in the cigarette. Show it to your silent audience and then untie it. Unroll the package, remove the cigarette, and your friend can smoke it without a bit of trouble. A little wrinkled, perhaps, but all in one piece.

Step and Kick

You're going to be delighted watching people try this one. Show them what is to be done by crossing your right leg behind your left and placing the end of a broom handle on your right toes. Now take one step with your left foot and then kick the broom across the room with your right. With a little practice you can propel it quite a distance and, at the same time, make it look very simple. Some of your students will find it difficult to get into position (some people are real klutzes, right?), and others will get a surprise by kicking their left foot right out from under themselves. It's a funny world.

When you practice the maneuver, it helps if you bend the left knee a little as you kick with your right foot.

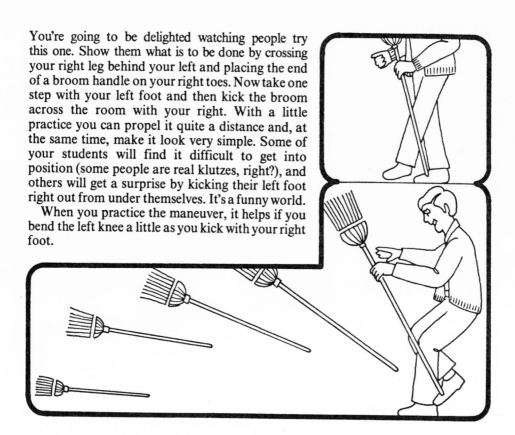

Forward and Backward

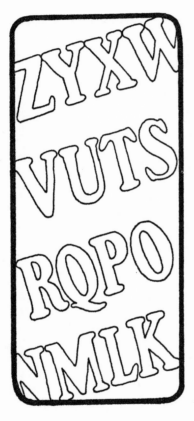

To show the benefit of higher education and a broad understanding of the failings of others, you propose a contest. You and the student will each take a pencil and paper. At someone's signal you will each write the English alphabet, but you will write yours backward and do so at least as fast as the student writes his forward. The signal is given, you both start, and sure enough, you not only match him for speed but in many cases actually finish first.

The way to learn this is to think of the backward alphabet as a series of foreign words. It works especially well if you break them into groups of four: ZYXW vuts RQPO nmlk JIHG fedc BA. Now try pronouncing them so you can fix them in your mind: zikswa, vutts, erkpo, nimlek, jig, fedec, bah. Step two is to think of each word as you write it, writing as fast as you can. In a surprisingly short time you'll be writing the entire alphabet, backward, as fast as your fingers will move.

Actually, you have two additional things working for you. Most adults still don't have their alphabet down perfectly and they'll have to stop and think during their scribbling. Also, they are used to writing words, not the alphabet, and you are!

Oh, yes, if you think you have a formidable adversary on your hands you can inject a very sly psychological trick into the performance. As you're writing the alphabet backward, say the alphabet out loud, but forward. Even though you're naming the letters in the same direction as he's writing, it will confuse his abc's. But don't forget to practice it beforehand.

Calendar Memory

"What do you mean you still need a calendar to see what day of the week your birthday is on? Your memory must be terrible. I know the day for every date through December 31, 1986. What do you mean, that would take a photographic memory? There's nothing to it. Listen, give me your birth date and I'll tell you which day of the week it is."

And it's true, you can give the day of the week for any day of the year. For example, if someone wants to know which day of the week April 16th was, you think for a few seconds and name Monday as the day. And you're right!

Actually, all you have to do is memorize the date of the first Sunday of each month. Now the first Sunday of January 1984 was on the first day of the month, in February it was on the fifth, and in March it was on the fourth. So if we list the first Sundays by number we have—

1	5	4	1	6	3
JAN	FEB	MAR	APR	MAY	JUN
1	5	2	7	4	2
JUL	AUG	SEP	OCT	NOV	DEC

Now let's put them in a more easily memorized form:

154-163
152-742

Think of them as two very simplified telephone numbers; after all, there is one less digit in these numbers. Notice that we've put them in groups of three so that you can easily find each month; January is the first month, February is second, and so on. Suppose someone asks for, say, the 10th of August. Looking at our "telephone numbers" in our memory we find the digit for August is 1. So starting with 1, the first Sunday, the second Sunday must be the 8th. Then count 9 and 10 (Monday and Tuesday). Therefore, the 10th of August was a Tuesday. With the same procedure we look for the 17th of June. Its first Sunday was on the 6th, add 7 to that to get the second Sunday on the 13th, and then count along the days of the week—14, 15, 16, 17 . . . it's Thursday.

For 1977 you use the following:

    266 - 315
    374 - 264

And 1978 is—

    155 - 274
    263 - 153

Happy dating!

Billiards Basketball

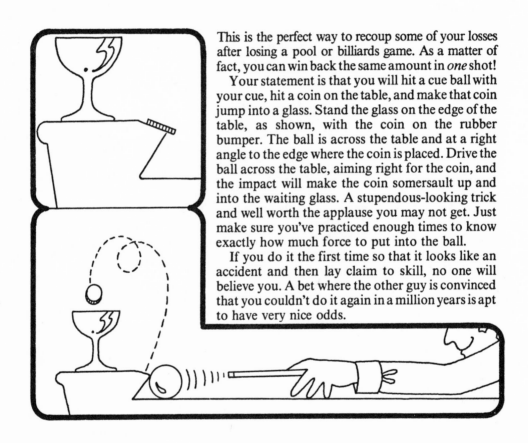

This is the perfect way to recoup some of your losses after losing a pool or billiards game. As a matter of fact, you can win back the same amount in *one* shot!

Your statement is that you will hit a cue ball with your cue, hit a coin on the table, and make that coin jump into a glass. Stand the glass on the edge of the table, as shown, with the coin on the rubber bumper. The ball is across the table and at a right angle to the edge where the coin is placed. Drive the ball across the table, aiming right for the coin, and the impact will make the coin somersault up and into the waiting glass. A stupendous-looking trick and well worth the applause you may not get. Just make sure you've practiced enough times to know exactly how much force to put into the ball.

If you do it the first time so that it looks like an accident and then lay claim to skill, no one will believe you. A bet where the other guy is convinced that you couldn't do it again in a million years is apt to have very nice odds.

Rolling Home

This last demonstration also takes place on a pool table. You state flat out that you can roll a wine glass across a pool table and sink it in a pocket. There will be doubtful looks, thoughtful looks, and some downright sneers, but stick to your guns and someone will take you up on it.

In practice you have done the trick in reverse by putting the base of the wine glass over the pocket and then rolling it away from the pocket. This tells you where to place the glass when you do the trick. Put the glass at that spot, place your flat hand on it from above, and firmly push it away from the edge. It will make a beautiful long arc and drop neatly into the pocket.

End of game!

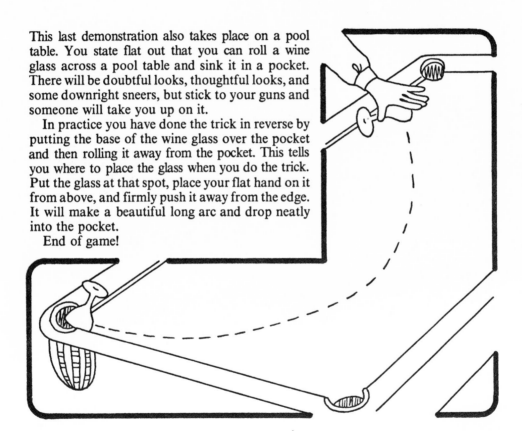

Cork Challenge

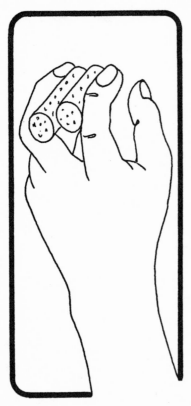

Have you ever picked up the wine corks from the dinner table and wondered what you could do with them? Well, here's an answer that could garner you some wonderful publicity or, even more wonderful, something of value.

Stand two wine corks side by side on the table and challenge anyone to pick them up, just by using the index and middle finger of one hand.

People will try, but all they will accomplish is having the corks roll out of their fingers and across the table. When it comes to your turn, form your hand into a loose fist with the first two fingers extended. Place one finger on each side of the two corks and just as you squeeze the two fingers together, put a slight curve in them. This curve will let the tips of your fingers lock the two corks together, and you'll be able to lift them with ease.

8. Figuring the Odds
Coins, Dice, Cards, and Numbers

No matter how hard you talk to a pair of dice, they just can't hear you. A coin has no idea whether it came up heads or tails on the last flip, and, regardless of your prayers, a deck of cards doesn't arrange itself to alternate high and low cards, or red or black, to accommodate the player. But though the cards, the coins, and dice are dumb, it doesn't mean that you need to be.

This chapter will give you the opportunity to learn how to figure odds and understand how probability works. It isn't difficult. The mathematics of it all has been known for centuries. I'll give you examples of what I mean each time we change subject or take a look at a different method of figuring odds, so you will have a good understanding of why certain bets are good and others are bad. I'll also give you some bets to use at your next gathering of students. It will make them wish they had paid a little more attention in math class.

For example, take a penny from your pocket and flip it a few times in front of a friend. Ask him if you flipped the coin nine times and it came up heads nine times in a row, what the odds are of it coming up heads again on the tenth flip? Nine times out of

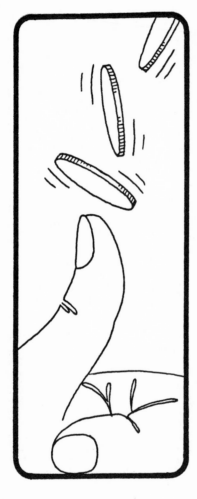

ten, he'll do some serious thinking and then say 9-to-1, but he's wrong. The true odds are 1-to-1. Why?

Remember, the coin can't think for itself. It can only come up heads or tails. Those are the only two possibilities. If you're betting on each single flip of the coin, then you have one favorable possibility and one unfavorable, no matter what has happened in the prior tosses. This is the key to figuring probability, the number of unfavorable against the favorable. In the case of a coin they are always 1-to-1.

Flipping a single coin can be interesting, but to make things really exciting take a second one out of your pocket. Now, what are the possibilities when you're tossing two coins? Since the results can be two heads, two tails, or one of each, does that mean there are three possibilities? No. Actually there are four combinations. Remember, you have to consider each possibility of each object combined with each possibility of the other objects involved. So, in reality, we can get:

Head on #1 and tail on #2
Tail on #1 and head on #2
Head on #1 and head on #2
Tail on #1 and tail on #2

Not three combinations, but four. This means that you have two chances out of four of tossing one head and one tail. That's even money, but in tossing either both heads or both tails, the chances are 3-1 against you.

Each time you add a coin, you add to the number of possibilities. This takes us into the subject of permutations. What are permutations? Well, a permutation is the total number of ways a combination of possibilities can be arranged. For example, you can only arrange an apple and an orange in a line two ways: either the apple first and then the orange, or the orange first and then the apple. Three items can be arranged in six permutations. Take the colors red, white, and blue. They can be arranged red/white/blue, white/blue/red, blue/red/white, blue/white/red, white/red/blue, and red/blue/white.

The way you figure these permutations is very easy. If there are only two items, then you multiply 2x1 to get the number of combinations; if there are three, you multiply 3x2x1; and if there are four, you multiply 4x3x2x1; and so on. You very quickly get into some very large numbers. Let me show you how quickly the digits mount up. If you use factorial 10 (the mathematical term for this type of computation), the answer is 3,628,800, while factorial 20 is 2,432,902,008,176,640,000. To eliminate the need of writing all these long and involved numbers, the probability experts use an exclamation point to denote the factorial use of a number. So, while 5! is equal to 120, 52! will have 68 digits. Keep this particular factorial number in mind, because we're going to be using it for a number of the playing card betchas.

Way back in the 1650's Blaise Pascal was given the problem of figuring out some gambling odds. Out of his calculations came Pascal's Triangle.

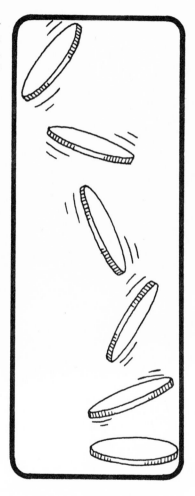

Now, Pascal's Triangle is a graphic picture of permutations. Each level of the triangle has a 1 at each end, and each of the other triangles in that line is the sum of the two triangles in the line just above it. Each level gives the total of possibilities involving coins or other 1-to-1 chances. The third level gives you a total of 8, the number of chances with three coins. Starting at the left and reading to the right, you can read the different combinations: one chance of all three coins being heads, three chances of two heads and one tail, three chances of one head and two tails, and one chance of all three being tails. Read each level in this manner, starting with heads at the left, and eliminating one head and adding one tail each time you move to the right.

What if you don't have one of Pascal's Tricky Triangles in your pocket when you need to know the number of permutations of a number of coins? That's easy, too. You just multiply the digit 2 (the number of possibilities on a coin) by itself equal to the number of coins. In other words, if you want to know the number of permutations of four coins, you would just multiply 2 by itself four times:

$$2\times2\times2\times2 = 16 \text{ permutations.}$$

How do you use all this in day-to-day combat? Well, line up a student and see if he can figure out a simple bet. Give him three coins and have him toss them into the air. Tell him that if they come up with three heads or three tails, you'll pay him 2-to-1. But, you add, if they come up with two heads or two tails, he's to pay you even money. "In other words,"

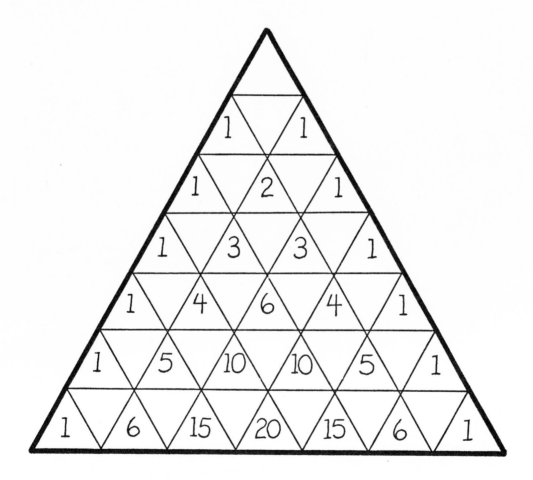

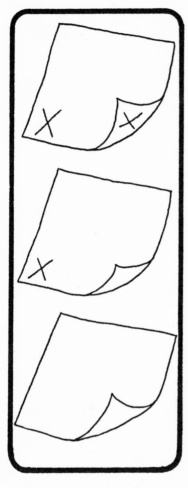

you say slowly, "you have a 50-50 chance, but I'll pay double."

You'll have fun watching him try to work his way through all the blue smoke, but the odds are that he'll finally take you up on it. Actually, as you can now figure out in your head, the odds against him are 3-to-1.

The trick is to remember to keep track of all the possibilities. Take three pieces of blank paper. Mark one with an X on each side, mark the second with an X on just one side, and leave the third card blank. Have a student put them in a paper bag and shake so no one knows which card is where. Reach into the bag, remove one card, and place it on the table without looking at the other side. Suppose an X is showing. You say, "Obviously, this isn't the card that is blank on both sides, so it has to be one of the other two cards. I'll bet even money that this is the card that has an X on both sides."

Is it a good bet? Actually, the odds are 2-to-1 in your favor. If the card on the table is the X/blank card, that's one possibility, and if it's one side of the X/X card then that is a second possibility. But it could also be the other side of the X/X card, and that makes three possibilities. Two-to-one, right? In other words, of the three unseen sides (remember you eliminated one card), two of them match the side now showing.

Let's apply the same logic to a game of cards. You are playing poker and you have three Spades in your dealt hand. You have an overpowering hunch to try for a Spade Flush; what are your chances?

You have five cards in your hand, so there are 47 left. Of those 47, 10 are Spades. So, the probability of drawing a Spade on the first card is 10/47 (10 Spades out of 47 possibilities). If that draw is favorable and you get a Spade, then the probability of getting another Spade on the second card you draw is now 9/46. So the answer of the probability of getting two Spades to fill your three-card Flush is expressed as:

$$\frac{10}{47} \times \frac{9}{46} = \frac{90}{2162} \quad \text{or 24-to-1 } (2162 \div 90 = 24)$$

Once you begin to understand how these things work, it really isn't that difficult.

Let's look at a pair of dice. There is absolutely nothing frightening about two little cubes of celluloid, but MILLIONS of dice players refuse to learn the odds against them. There's no need for you to be one of them.

Each die has six sides, numbered from 1 to 6, so you can tell them apart. If we pair the 1 on this die with each of the six sides of the other die, we get six different totals. If we do the same with the 2 on this die, we get six more totals. Therefore, we take six sides on one die times the six sides of the second die for a total of 36 combinations.

Here are those 36 combinations in chart form.

Out of these 36 combinations, there is only one way to make the number 2 and this is with the Ace of each die. A 3 can be made in two ways, and a 4 in

2=

3=

4=

5=

6=

7=

8=

9=

10=

11=

12=

132

three ways. This continues until you find six ways to make the number 7, and then the possibilities begin to decrease. This simple chart is the ruling factor of any dice proposition. If you learn this one simple principle, you immediately begin to understand the so-called complexities of craps, chuck-a-luck, yahtze, or any other dice game.

In the game of craps you bet on the possibility of the shooter making his point before rolling a 7. The points are 4, 5, 6, 8, 9, and 10. Here are the odds on rolling one of them, rather than a 7:

$$4 - 2\text{-to-}1$$
$$5 - 3\text{-to-}2$$
$$6 - 6\text{-to-}5$$
$$8 - 6\text{-to-}5$$
$$9 - 3\text{-to-}2$$
$$10 - 2\text{-to-}1$$

Why are 4 and 10 2-to-1 bets? Because by referring to that chart of combinations, you see there are six ways to make a 7 (a bad number in this case) and only three ways to make a 4; therefore, the unfavorable odds against the favorable odds are 6-to-3 or 2-to-1. This same principle applies to all of the other points as well. There are six ways to make a 7, but only five ways for a 6, so it's a 6-to-5 bet. An 8 isn't an even money bet, but it is better than a 4.

See how simple it all is?

With these combinations in mind, let's look at some dice propositions that sound fairly straight, but aren't really what they seem.

Rolling 5 or 9 Before 7

You can safely bet someone that you will roll either a 5 *or* a 9 before you roll a 7. There are four ways to make the 5 and four ways to make the 9, only six ways for the 7. Therefore, the odds are 6-to-8, or 3-to-4 in your favor.

Rolling 6 or 1

Give someone a pair of dice and bet them that they will come up with either a 6 or a 1 on each roll. This is a super bet, because the student figures that with two numbers out of six on each die, maybe you have a 2-to-1 odds against you; or even if he made a slight mistake in figuring the odds, he should still have an even money bet. But look on the combination chart and count the pairs of dice that have an Ace or 6 or both. You'll find 20 out of the 36. That gives you a 5-to-9 edge. Big enough for you? Notice that any other combination of two numbers will also pop up 20 out of 36 times.

We Match

Cards, like dice and coins, yield some startling results. Shuffle one pack of cards while your student shuffles a second deck. When ready, bet him that as the two of you together deal cards faceup onto the table, somewhere in those 52 cards you will both deal the same card at the same time. In other words, you might both turn up the Four of Spades or the Six of Diamonds or some other card at the same time.

Sound good? I hope to tell you it is, and you'll always get a bet, because everybody wants to find the gimmick to it. You might even grumble a bit to get 2-to-1 odds. Actually, you already have 20-to-1 odds in your favor. How do we know? Well, this one takes a little effort to figure out, but let me point you in the right direction. Take the fraction 51/52 (51 possibilities out of 52 of missing on each card dealt); if you multiply it by itself for 52 times, you will come up with a very long fraction that reduces to about 1/3. Meaning, of course, that you will miss about once every three times you try it.

Two-Card Flush

Your willing student shuffles the deck, and then divides it into three piles of cards in front of you. Before you turn over the top card of each pile, you bet him there will be two cards of the same suit showing. "Four suit . . . only three cards . . . I shuffle the deck"—everything sounds good to the student. So he goes for the bet, and you go with his money.

Instead of trying to work out a formula for this one, just say it backwards and see if you would take a chance on it. "Turn over three cards and try to get three different suits without a match." Doesn't sound so good, does it? That's because it's a little more obvious that the odds are against you.

Ace, Two, Three . . .

Have your student shuffle the deck, cut it, and then set it in front of you. Bet him that as you deal cards faceup onto the table, calling out, "Ace, two, three, four . . . ," and so on, through the values, you will correctly call out one card as you turn it over.

This one is really loaded in your favor. Try it once for practice. After you have made a correct match continue on through the deck. You'll find others that also match. I've counted as many as six or seven in one run-through.

Five Pat Hands

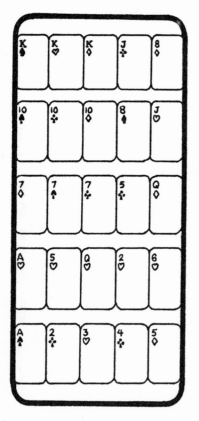

Here's a good one that doesn't involve odds at all. As someone shuffles a deck of cards, tell him you're so used to looking at poker hands that you can even make 5 pat poker hands (Three-of-a-Kind or better) out of 25 miscellaneous cards. When he takes you up on it at even money, have him deal 25 cards faceup onto the table. Arrange them into 5 rows of 5 cards each, and then start looking for your combinations. To make your work easy as possible, look first for all the Three-of-a-Kind combinations, which will probably work out to give you three of your hands. Now look for a Flush among the remaining 16 cards, and then see if you can make up a Straight. It's very seldom that you can't finish up the last hand.

Calling Three Cards

This little betcha is very interesting. I've heard it for years, and I know it is a very powerful bet. But when I wanted to figure out the odds on why it works, the numbers didn't come out as strong as the results when I actually tried it. So, I took the simple problem to a probabilities professor at a West Coast university. After two weeks he was still struggling with the problem. I know it can be figured. Any problem can. But what's the answer? If you figure it out, let me know, will you?

Have someone call out any three card values, like Ace, Queen, and Nine. Bet him you can find two of those values together somewhere in the shuffled deck. Sounds like a longshot, doesn't it? But it isn't. Not for you. I've found as many as four winning combinations in one run-through of the pack. Try it for yourself.

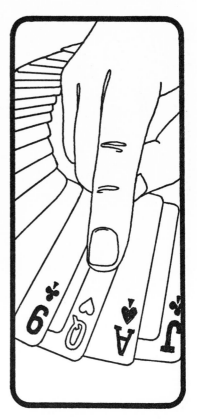

Happy Unbirthday

In a group of 30 people, bet your student that among them are two individuals with the same birthday. He'll think about the 30 people with the 365 possibilities and, unless he read this book before you did, will jump at the chance to prove you wrong. Well, check the dates and then take his money, because you have a 70 percent chance of winning.

Why? Well, this one is figured like the other permutations, with one exception. You start with the fraction 364/365 (the number of dates left after the first person names his birthdate) and multiply it by 363/365 (the number left after the second person names his date), and then by 362/365, and continue on until you finish with 334/365 (the last person's date). Reducing this superlong fraction will give you approximately 7/10, or a damn good bet. If you want to strengthen the Law of Probability, then work with 50 people; you'll have a 40-to-1 edge in your favor. How's that for not taking a chance?

Make Book on It

If you're not at a party where you can easily re-search thirty birthdays, then use a telephone book. Let your student pick any page and any column of names. Have him mark off twenty consecutive telephone numbers in that column, and bet him that somewhere in those numbers there are two that have the same last two digits, like 52 or 37. Most people figure that the odds are about 100-to-1 against that chance, so they'll take you up on it. And lose!

The odds are actually 7-to-1 in your favor. You figure it the same way as the birthday bet; 99/100 times 98/100 times 97/100 and so on, for 20 fractions (one for each telephone number marked). This will come out to about 7/10 when reduced.

Booking Backwards

If, on that last bet, your friend starts complaining that you're taking advantage of him, tell him you'll not only reverse the bet but even increase the odds for him. Have him turn to another page and another column. This time put a check against the first name and check off the next fifty names. You bet him that the last two digits of the telephone number by the checked name are *not* duplicated in those next fifty numbers. If he doesn't jump at the chance, then send him home because right off the bat he should realize that you're letting him work with more than twice the numbers you had.

But he isn't! You've reworded the bet. Now the last two digits of the first number have to be matched against each of the following fifty. You've not only reversed the bet but you still have an edge, 3-to-2, in your favor. Reread the wording of the two versions, so you clearly understand the difference. In the first bet you are matching *all* the numbers against *each* other, and in the second you are matching *one* number against *all* the others.

Alphabetically Best

By this time your student may be complaining about the headache he's getting from the long string of numbers he has to work with. So, be kind. Switch to the alphabet. Anyone should be able to handle twenty-six letters, right? So have him write down any five letters of the alphabet he wishes, and tell him that you can guess at least one of them if he gives you five chances. If he has some friends with him, so much the better. You can take them all on at the same time. Just have each of them write down his choices, you'll use the same five guesses for all of them. What they don't know is that you'll probably win two out of the three bets. Just write down any five letters that pop into your head and reach for the money.

License Fee

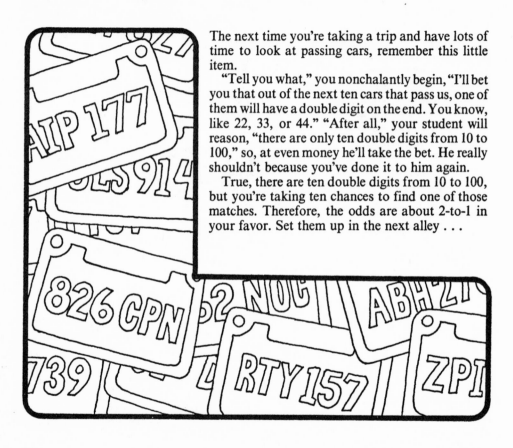

The next time you're taking a trip and have lots of time to look at passing cars, remember this little item.

"Tell you what," you nonchalantly begin, "I'll bet you that out of the next ten cars that pass us, one of them will have a double digit on the end. You know, like 22, 33, or 44." "After all," your student will reason, "there are only ten double digits from 10 to 100," so, at even money he'll take the bet. He really shouldn't because you've done it to him again.

True, there are ten double digits from 10 to 100, but you're taking ten chances to find one of those matches. Therefore, the odds are about 2-to-1 in your favor. Set them up in the next alley . . .

Calling Three Coins

What everyone knows is almost always wrong, and when it isn't wrong, it can still lead to some wonderfully enticing betchas.

Everyone knows when you flip a coin once, the odds are even as to whether it will come up heads or tails. This far everyone is right. But how many people could resist giving you odds if you were to say, "I'll bet when I toss this coin I can guess correctly two out of three times." After all, everybody knows that it's harder to be right two out of three times on an even money bet. Well, anybody who can't resist this inviting proposition will end up a loser. The fact is that this is still an even money bet, because one or the other of you will have to be right at least two out of three times. If you're not right, then the other person has to get two out of three.

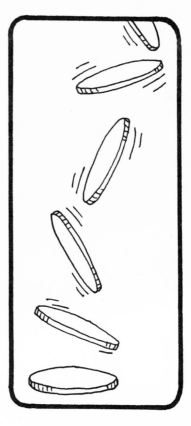

9. Getting Away with It

In spite of millions of years of the gradual improvement of the human species, there are still some people born with a genetic deficiency in their sense of humor.

Every now and then, into the life of even the most charming, wicked wagerer, there enters somebody who doesn't see the fun in the fun. I hope you do not know any such unfortunate humans, but if you come across one in the attempt to educate mankind in betchas, it's always a good idea to be prepared with an exit that will guarantee you an unfair head start.

With a little luck, you'll never need to call upon these devices, but by now we all know that luck has very little to do with most wagers and to depend upon it is to have a most unreliable friend.

The Emergency Egg-xit

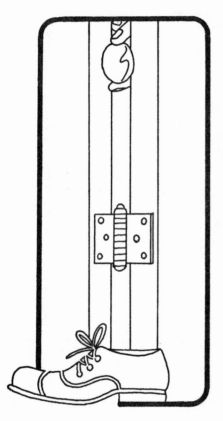

Sometimes you need something to get you out of a situation and you've run out of other possibilities. This one should do it.

Ask the student if he's confident of the strength in his fingers, and when you get his complete satisfaction then propose this little test. Bet him that he can't put his first two fingers through the crack of a door, between the door and the jamb on the hinge side, and be able to hold an egg gently enough to keep from breaking the shell.

As you're placing him behind the door, have him remove his shoes so he doesn't slip in the narrow space. When he has the egg firmly in his two-fingered grasp, place one of his shoes under the egg, and leave.

The Weakest Link

A chain is not supposed to be stronger than its weakest link, and if the weakest link is nothing more than ordinary thread, how strong can the chain be? Well, your student will discover the answer to this question the hard way.

Tell your student that you know how bright, charming, and attractive he is, but that the one thing that you question is his strength. Then remove a spool of thread from your pocket and show him how easy it is for you to break the thread between your hands. Now tell the student that you bet that you can tie him up with the thread so that he won't be able to move. When the student takes you up on the challenge, as he will, get him to bend over in the position pictured in the illustration and tie his thumbs together with a number of loops of the thread. He'll soon discover that it's one thing to break a thread between his hands and another to break it with his thumbs.

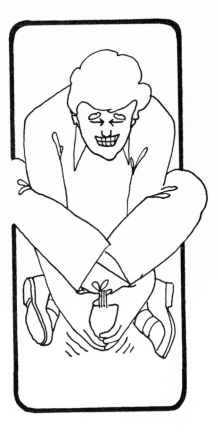